200 delicious desserts

200 delicious desserts

hamlyn **all color**

Sara Lewis

For Sian, a few ideas to help broaden your repertoire!

An Hachette UK Company
www.hachette.co.uk

First published in Great Britain in 2009 by
Hamlyn, a division of Octopus Publishing Group Ltd,
2–4 Heron Quays, London E14 4JP
www.octopusbooksusa.com

Distributed in the U.S. and Canada by Octopus Books USA:
c/o Hachette Book Group
237 Park Avenue
New York NY 10017

Some of the recipes in this book have previously appeared
in other books published by Hamlyn.

ISBN: 978-0-600-62015-0

A CIP catalog record for this book is available from
the Library of Congress.

Printed and bound in China

1 2 3 4 5 6 7 8 9 10

Standard level spoon measurements are used in all recipes

Ovens should be preheated to the specified temperature—if
using a fan-assisted oven, follow the manufacturer's
instructions for adjusting the time and the temperature.

Milk should be whole milk unless otherwise stated.

Eggs should be medium unless otherwise stated. The Food
and Drug Adminstration advises that eggs should not be
consumed raw. This book contains some dishes made with
raw or lightly cooked eggs. It is prudent for vulnerable people
such as pregnant and nursing mothers, invalids, the elderly,
babies, and young children to avoid uncooked or lightly
cooked dishes made with eggs. Once prepared, these dishes
should be kept refrigerated and used promptly.

This book also includes dishes made with nuts and nut
derivatives. It is advisable for those with known allergic
reactions to nuts and nut derivatives and those who may be
potentially vulnerable to these allergies, such as pregnant and
nursing mothers, invalids, the elderly, babies, and children to
avoid dishes made with nuts and nut oils. It is also prudent
to check the labels of pre-prepared ingredients for the possible
inclusion of nut derivatives.

contents

introduction

introduction

Not many people can resist a dessert. A good one will cheer you up after a bad day at work, banish the blues, and make a grand finale to a special meal or a welcome alternative gift to a bunch of flowers when visiting friends for supper. And with over 200 recipes in this book, there's something here for everyone.

Those who need a chocolate fix can choose from such decadent delights as Double Chocolate Puddings (see page 38), hot from the oven and drizzled with white chocolate cream, or a slice of rich gooey Chocolate & Marshmallow Torte (see page 42). If you're a pastry fan, try the melt in-the-mouth Freeform Apple & Mixed Berry Pie (see page 70) or the Deep Dish Puff Apple Pie (see page 90). Alternatively, if you are watching your weight, there are even healthy

fresh-fruit recipes, such the Green Fruit Salad (see page 204).

Short of time? You can cheat and use store-bought puff or sweet shortcrust pastry to make impressive desserts like Peach & Blueberry Jalousie (see page 64), Cherry Frangipane Tart (see page 82), or the comforting Lemon Meringue Pie (see page 74). Even easier is a cookie crumb case, such as Banoffee Pie (see page 108). There's a whole chapter called "Last-minute Quickies," full of ideas for desserts that can be whipped up in no more than 10–20 minutes, such as Tamarind & Mango Sundae (see page 200) or Mini Baked Alaskas (see page 218).

If you like to get organized in advance, try one of the frozen recipes in the "Chilled Out" chapter, such as Lime & Passion Fruit Crunch Tart (see page 164) or Mint Granita (see page 180). These ice-cold treats are perfect after a barbecue in the garden or a hot curry in the winter.

These days, our busy schedules mean a homemade dessert is a treat rather than an everyday occurrence, but when you do have the time to make one it is not only immensely rewarding but also a great way to unwind.

Pages 9–14 describe the dessert-making techniques: beating eggs and sugar, folding in, working with chocolate, making meringues, lining a pie shell, and decorating a pie. On page 15 you'll find recipes for homemade flaky and sweet shortcrust pastry.

beating eggs and sugar

When making mousses, chilled soufflés, sabayon sauce, zabaglione, a jelly roll, or a cake shell, the recipe will call for the eggs and sugar to be beaten until the whisk leaves a trail when lifted above the mixture. This is best done with a hand-held electric mixer held over a bowl of eggs and sugar set over a saucepan of gently simmering water. The hot water helps to speed up the beating process and increase the volume of air trapped in the eggs and sugar. (If you have a fixed mixer, do this on the work surface; it will just take a little longer.)

Three eggs will take 8–10 minutes to beat until thick. To test when the mixture is ready, lift the whisk out of the mixture and try to drizzle a zigzag as the mixture falls from the whisk—if this stays on the surface for a few seconds, the mixture is ready.

whipping cream

Many people tend to overwhip heavy or whipping cream. The secret is to whip the cream until it just begins to form soft swirls, as it will thicken slightly as it stands. Overwhipping makes the cream take on a grainy, almost buttery texture and spoils the finish of the dessert.

folding in

Once a beaten mixture is ready, you will need to fold in pureed fruit, whipped cream, or melted chocolate for a chilled soufflé or mousse, or sifted flour for a sponge cake.

Use a large-bowled spoon (a serving spoon is ideal) and gently cut and turn the spoon through the mixture in a figure-of-eight movement. Try to be as gentle as you can so that you don't knock out all the air you have just worked so hard to incorporate.

making meringues

The bowl and whisk must both be dry and completely grease-free. If you drop any yolk at all into the whites when separating the eggs, scoop it out with a piece of shell, as even the tiniest amount of yolk will prevent the whites from thickening.

1 Beat the whites until very thick so they will stand in moist-looking peaks. If you're not sure whether they're ready, turn the bowl upside down—if the egg whites stay put, they're ready; if they begin to slide or fall out, beat a little more.

2 Gradually beat in the sugar a teaspoonful at a time. It may sound a slow process, but it makes for very thick meringue. When all the sugar has been added, beat for a couple of minutes more until the meringue is very thick and glossy.

3 Shape the meringues by spooning or spreading onto a baking sheet lined with nonstick parchment paper, and bake according to the recipe until the meringues are crisp and may be easily lifted off the paper. If they stick to the paper, they aren't ready. Return to the oven for 10–20 minutes and test again.

working with chocolate

To melt chocolate, break it into pieces and heat for 5 minutes or so in a bowl set over a saucepan of very gently simmering water, making sure that the water doesn't touch the base of the bowl. Stir just before using.

Decorative chocolate curls are easy to make using a swivel-bladed vegetable peeler. Place a chocolate bar on a cutting board with the smooth underside uppermost. Run the vegetable peeler blade along the top of the chocolate with the handle almost touching the edge of the bar. If the curls are very small, warm the chocolate in 10-second bursts in the microwave on full power (or in a warm oven) and try again. As the chocolate softens, the curls will increase in size.

lining a pie shell

A removable-based tart pan makes it easy to remove the finished tart after baking.

1 Roll out the pastry on a lightly floured surface until a little larger than the pan.

2 Lift the pastry over a rolling pin and drape into the pan. Press over the base and up the pan sides with your fingertips, taking care where the sides meet the base of the pan.

3 Trim off the excess pastry with a rolling pin or small knife, then press the pastry slightly above the top of the pan. Chill for 15 minutes or longer if you have time, to minimize shrinkage before cooking.

11

baking blind

This rather strange term really just means to bake the pie shell empty.

1 Stand the tart pan on a baking sheet, then prick the pastry base with a fork.

2 Line with crumpled nonstick or waxed paper. Half-fill the pan with dried macaroni or pie weights to hold the pastry in shape.

3 Bake at 375°F for 10–15 minutes until just set, then lift out the paper and filling. Cook the empty tart for 5 more minutes until golden around the top edges and the base is dry and crisp, or for 10 more minutes if the filling will not be cooked.

covering and decorating a pie

For a professional finish to a puff, flaky, or shortcrust topped fruit pie.

1 Cut a narrow strip of pastry from the edges of the rolled-out dough the same width as the rim of the pie dish. Brush the dish rim with water, beaten egg, or milk and stick the strips in place, butting ends of strips together until the rim is completely covered.

2 Lift the remaining pastry over a rolling pin and drape over the top of the pie. Press the edges together then trim off the excess pastry with a small knife.

3 Knock up the edges of the pie by making small horizontal cuts around the pastry rim. This helps to encourage the puff pastry layers to separate and rise during baking and can also give the impression of layers in a shortcrust pie.

4 Flute the edges by pressing the first and second finger onto the pie edge, then make small cuts with a knife between them to create a scalloped edge. Repeat all the way around the pie.

5 Brush the pie with a little beaten egg or milk to glaze it. To decorate with pastry leaves, roll out trimmings, cut a strip about 1 inch wide, then cut out diamond shapes. Mark veins with a knife and curl the ends of the leaf. Press onto the glazed pie, then brush over a little more glazing.

6 Alternatively, hearts, circles, festive shapes, or numbers can be stamped from rerolled pastry trimmings with small cookie cutters, then arranged on the glazed pie and glazed with a little more beaten egg or milk.

sweet shortcrust pastry

A great all-round pastry, versatile and quick to make, sweet shortcrust is ideal for pie shells, freeform pies, or double-crust pies. This recipe makes enough to fill a 10 inch tart pan or 14½ oz pastry.

2 cups **all-purpose flour**, plus extra for dusting
¼ cup **confectioners' sugar**
½ cup **unsalted butter** and **white vegetable shortening**, or all butter, diced
8–9 teaspoons cold **water**

Place the flour and sugar in a bowl, add the sugar and diced fats, and blend the fats into the flour by lifting up small amounts with the fingers and thumbs and pressing the thumbs over the fingertips to break the fats into tiny pieces. Continue until the mixture resembles fine bread crumbs. (For speed, use an electric mixer or food processor.) Add 8 teaspoons cold water and mix with a round-bladed knife until the crumbs begin to clump together, then squeeze with the fingertips, adding an extra teaspoon of water if needed to bring the mixture together to a ball. Knead lightly on a lightly floured surface then chill, wrapped in plastic wrap, for 15 minutes, or if preferred roll out, line a tart pan, and chill. If chilled, the pastry relaxes and shrinks less when baked.

flaky pastry

Supermarket puff pastry is so good, and homemade puff pastry so hard to get right, that it is not really worth making it yourself. Flaky pastry is much quicker and easier to make and this light crumbly pastry is perfect to top a deep-dish pie (such as Deep Dish Puff Apple Pie, see page 90) or to use for a jalousie-style double-crust pie or for individual pastries. This recipe makes enough to top a 5 cup pie dish or 1 lb pastry.

2 cups **all-purpose flour**, plus extra for dusting
pinch **salt**
⅓ cup **lard** or **white pastry shortening**
⅓ cup **unsalted butter**
2 teaspoons **lemon juice**
5–6 tablespoons cold **water**

Place the flour and salt in a mixing bowl, add one quarter of the white fat and one quarter of the butter, and blend in with the fingertips until the mixture resembles fine bread crumbs. Add the lemon juice then enough cold water, mixing with a round-bladed knife, to form a soft but not sticky dough. Knead lightly, then roll out on a floured surface to form a rough rectangle, about 18 x 6 inches. Dot half the remaining white fat and butter over the bottom two-thirds of the pastry. Fold over the top one-third of the dough and then fold up the bottom third to enclose the fat. Press the edges together well, then give the dough a quarter turn. Roll out the pastry again, dot with fats, and fold, as before. Give a quarter turn, then roll and fold twice more. Wrap in plastic wrap and chill for 30 minutes.

winter warmers

lemon puddle pudding

Serves **4**
Preparation time **20 minutes**
Cooking time **25 minutes**

⅓ cup **unsalted butter**, at
   room temperature
⅔ cup **superfine sugar**
grated zest of **2 lemons**, plus
   juice from 1 lemon
3 **eggs**, separated
½ cup **self-rising flour**
1¼ cups **milk**
confectioners' sugar, for
   dusting (optional)

Grease a 5 cup pie dish lightly, then stand the dish in a roasting pan. Put the rest of the butter in a mixing bowl with the sugar and lemon zest. Beat the egg whites in a separate bowl until they are softly peaking. Using the still dirty whisk, beat the butter, sugar, and lemon zest until light and fluffy, then mix in the flour and egg yolks.

Mix in the milk and lemon juice gradually until only just mixed. The mixture may appear to separate slightly but this will disappear during baking.

Fold in the egg whites, then gently pour the mix into the greased dish. Pour hot water from the tap into the roasting pan to come halfway up the sides of the dish.

Cook in a preheated oven, 375°F, for 25 minutes or until slightly risen and golden brown, and the top has begun to crack. Insert a knife into the center—the top two-thirds should be soufflé-like and the bottom third a saucy, custard-like layer. If it's very soft in the center, cook for an extra 5 minutes.

Dust the top with a little sifted confectioners' sugar, if desired, then serve immediately spooned into shallow bowls. Don't leave the dessert to stand or the topping will absorb the sauce.

For Grand Marnier pudding, use the grated zest of 1 large orange instead of the lemon zest and replace the lemon juice with 3 tablespoons Grand Marnier. Cook as above.

roasted pears with asian spices

Serves **4**
Preparation time **20 minutes**
Cooking time **25 minutes**

4 **pears**
8 tablespoons **dry** or **sweet sherry**
8 tablespoons **water**
6–8 pieces **star anise**
1 **cinnamon stick**, broken into pieces
8 **cloves**
8 **cardamom pods**, crushed
¼ cup **unsalted butter**
4 tablespoons **light brown sugar**
1 **orange**

Leave the peel on the pears and cut them in half, down through the stems to the base. Scoop out the core, then put in a roasting pan with the cut sides up. Spoon the sherry into the core cavity of each pear and the water into the base of the pan. Sprinkle the spices over the pears, including the cardamom pods and their black seeds. Dot with the butter, then sprinkle with the sugar.

Remove the zest from the orange and sprinkle into the pan. Cut the orange into wedges and squeeze the juice over the pears. Add the wedges to the base of the roasting pan.

Cook in a preheated oven, 350°F, for 25 minutes until tender and just beginning to brown, spooning the pan juices over the pears halfway through cooking and again at the end.

Spoon into shallow dishes, drizzle with the pan juices, and serve with crème fraîche or whole milk yogurt.

For roast apples with peppercorns, core and halve 4 dessert apples, then place, cut side up, in a roasting pan. Spoon ¾ cup hard cider over the apples and into the roasting pan. Sprinkle with 1 teaspoon coarsely crushed multicolored peppercorns and 1 broken cinnamon stick. Dot with butter and sprinkle with sugar as above. Remove the zest from 1 lemon and reserve for decoration, then cut the lemon into wedges, squeeze the juice over the apples, and add the wedges to the base of the pan. Bake as above.

sticky toffee puddings

Makes **8**
Preparation time **20 minutes**
Cooking time **45–50 minutes**

⅔ cup pitted chopped **dried dates**
⅔ cup **water**
½ cup **unsalted butter**, softened
½ cup **superfine sugar**
1 teaspoon **vanilla extract**
3 **eggs**
1½ cups **self-rising flour**
1 teaspoon **baking powder**

Toffee sauce
1¼ cups **heavy cream**
½ cup **light brown sugar**
¼ cup **unsalted butter**

Put the dates in a small pan with the measured water and simmer gently for 5 minutes until the dates are soft and pulpy. Blend to a puree, then allow to cool.

Make the sauce. Heat half the cream in a small, heavy pan with the sugar and butter until the sugar dissolves. Bring to a boil, then let the sauce bubble for about 5 minutes until a rich, dark caramel. Stir in the rest of the cream and set aside.

Grease 8 metal ¾ cup pudding molds and line the bottoms with nonstick parchment paper. Beat the butter, sugar, vanilla extract, eggs, flour, and baking powder in a bowl for 1–2 minutes until pale and creamy. Stir the date puree into the pudding mixture.

Divide the mixture among the molds. Level the tops and place in a roasting pan. Pour boiling water to a depth of ¾ inch in the pan and cover with foil. Bake in a preheated oven, 350°F, for 35–40 minutes or until risen and firm to the touch.

Leave the puddings in the molds while you reheat the sauce, then loosen the edges of the molds and invert the puddings onto serving plates. Cover with sauce and serve with additional cream or ice cream.

For gingered figgy puddings, cook ⅔ cup diced dried figs in the water in place of the dates. Make the sauce and puddings as above, adding 2 tablespoons chopped candied ginger to the beaten pudding mix.

choco bread & butter pudding

Serves **4**

Preparation time **20 minutes**, plus standing

Cooking time **25 minutes**

4 **chocolate croissants**

¼ cup **unsalted butter**

¼ cup **superfine sugar**

¼ teaspoon **ground mixed spice**

1¼ cups **milk**

4 **eggs**

1 teaspoon **vanilla extract**

confectioners' sugar, to decorate

Grease a 5 cup shallow, round, ovenproof pie dish. Slice the croissants thickly and spread the butter over one side of each cut face of croissant. Stand the croissant slices upright and close together in the dish to completely fill it.

Mix the sugar and spice together, then spoon over the croissants and between the gaps. Stand the dish in a large roasting pan.

Beat the milk, eggs, and vanilla extract together, then strain into the dish. Allow to stand for 15 minutes.

Pour hot water from the tap into the roasting pan to come halfway up the sides of the pie dish. Bake in a preheated oven, 350°F, for about 25 minutes until the pudding is golden and the custard just set.

Lift the dish out of the roasting pan, dust with sifted confectioners' sugar, and serve the pudding warm with a little pouring cream.

For fruited bread & butter pudding, lightly butter 8 slices of white bread, cut into triangles, and arrange in slightly overlapping layers in the dish, sprinkling with ½ cup luxury dried fruit between the layers. Add the sugar as above, but omit the mixed spice. Mix the eggs, milk, and vanilla, pour over the bread, then continue as above.

hot blackberry & apple trifle

Serves **4**
Preparation time **20 minutes**,
  plus cooling
Cooking time **20–25 minutes**

1 cup **fresh** or **frozen
  blackberries**
2 **dessert apples**, cored,
  unpeeled, and sliced
1 tablespoon **water**
¼ cup **superfine sugar**
4 slices **pound cake**
3 tablespoons **dry** or **sweet
  sherry**
14 oz can or carton **custard**

Meringue
3 **egg whites**
⅓ cup **superfine sugar**

Put the blackberries, apples, measured water, and sugar in a saucepan, then cover and simmer for 5 minutes or until the fruit has softened. Allow the mixture to cool slightly.

Break the cake slices into chunks and arrange in an even layer in the base of a 5 cup ovenproof pie or soufflé dish and drizzle with the sherry. Spoon the poached fruit and syrup over the top, then cover with custard.

Beat the egg whites in a large, dry bowl until stiffly peaking, then gradually beat in the sugar, a teaspoonful at a time, until the meringue is stiff and glossy (see page 10). Spoon over the custard and swirl the top with the back of a spoon.

Bake in a preheated oven, 350°F, for 15–20 minutes until heated through and the meringue is golden, then serve immediately.

For apple mallow, peel, core, and thickly slice 8 dessert apples, then simmer in a saucepan with the grated zest and juice of 1 lemon, 4 cloves, and 2 tablespoons superfine sugar until tender. Spoon into a 5 cup ovenproof dish. Make the meringue as above, adding ¼ teaspoon ground cinnamon with the sugar. Spoon over the fruit, then bake as above. Serve the mallow warm.

vanilla soufflés & apricot coulis

Serves **8**
Preparation time **25 minutes**
Cooking time **25 minutes**

6 tablespoons **superfine sugar**, plus extra for dusting
1 cup **ready-to-eat dried apricots**, coarsely chopped
½ cup **water**, plus 1 tablespoon
3 tablespoons **cornstarch**
5 tablespoons **Cointreau** or other **orange-flavored liqueur**
⅔ cup **milk**
1 teaspoon **vanilla extract**
½ cup **heavy cream**
4 **eggs**, separated
confectioners' sugar, for dusting

Grease 8 ramekin dishes and dust lightly with superfine sugar. Put the apricots in a small pan with the measured water and simmer gently for 3 minutes until softened. Blend ½ teaspoon of the cornstarch with 1 tablespoon water and add it to the pan. Cook gently for 1 minute or until the sauce has thickened.

Put the mixture in a food processor or blender, add the liqueur, and blend until smooth. Divide the mixture among the ramekins.

Blend the remaining cornstarch in a pan with a little of the milk. Add the remaining milk and heat gently, stirring, until thickened. Stir in 4 tablespoons of the superfine sugar, the vanilla extract, cream, and egg yolks and put in a large bowl.

Beat the egg whites until peaking and gradually beat in the remaining superfine sugar. Using a large metal spoon, fold the egg whites into the custard.

Spoon the mixture into the ramekins and put them on a baking sheet. Bake in a preheated oven, 400°F, for 20 minutes or until well risen. Dust with sifted confectioners' sugar, then serve.

For apple & Calvados soufflés, peel, core, and dice 4 dessert apples. Place in a small saucepan with 2 tablespoons water, cover, and cook for 10 minutes until soft. Divide between 8 greased and sugared ramekins. Make the soufflés as above, adding 5 tablespoons Calvados or ordinary brandy instead of the Cointreau.

jelly roly-poly

Serves **6**
Preparation time **25 minutes**
Cooking time **2 hours**

2½ cups **self-rising flour**
1 teaspoon **baking powder**
1¼ cups **shredded vegetable suet**
⅓ cup **superfine sugar**
1 cup **fresh bread crumbs**
finely grated zest of 1 **lemon**
finely grated zest of 1 **orange**
1 **egg**, beaten
about ¾ cup **milk**
6 tablespoons **raspberry jelly**
1¼ cups **frozen raspberries**, just defrosted

Put the flour, baking powder, suet, and sugar in a bowl, then stir in the bread crumbs and fruit zests. Add the egg, then gradually mix in enough milk to make a soft but not sticky dough.

Knead lightly, then roll out to a 12 inch square. Spread with the jelly, leaving a 1 inch border, then sprinkle the raspberries on top. Brush the border with a little milk, then roll up the pastry. Wrap loosely in a large piece of nonstick parchment paper, twisting the edges together and leaving a little space for the pudding to rise, then wrap loosely in foil.

Put on a roasting rack set over a large roasting pan, then pour boiling water into the pan but not over the roasting rack. Cover the pan with foil and twist over the edges to seal well, then bake in a preheated oven, 300°F, for 2 hours until the pudding is well risen. Check once or twice during baking and top up the water level if needed.

Transfer the pudding to a cutting board using a dish towel. Unwrap, cut into thick slices, and serve with hot custard.

For spotted dick, warm 3 tablespoons orange juice or rum in a small saucepan, add 1 cup raisins, 1 teaspoon ground ginger, and ¼ teaspoon grated nutmeg and allow to soak for 1 hour or longer. Add to the flour mix just before adding the egg and milk. Shape into a long sausage, wrap in paper and foil, and steam in the oven as above. Serve sliced with custard flavored with a little extra rum, if desired.

apricot queen of puddings

Serves **6**
Preparation time **25 minutes**,
  plus standing
Cooking time **35–45 minutes**

2½ cups **milk**
grated zest of 2 **lemons**
¼ cup **unsalted butter**
¾ cup **superfine sugar**
2 cups **fresh bread crumbs**
4 **eggs**, separated
4 tablespoons **apricot jelly**
⅔ cup ready-to-eat **dried
  apricots**, diced

Pour the milk into a saucepan, add the lemon zest, and bring just to a boil. Take off the heat and stir in the butter and ¼ cup of the sugar until the butter has melted and the sugar dissolved. Mix in the bread crumbs and allow to stand for 15 minutes.

Mix the egg yolks into the milk mixture, then pour into a greased 6 cup ovenproof pie dish. Bake in a preheated oven, 350°F, for 20–25 minutes until the custard has set and is just beginning to brown around the edges.

Dot the jelly over the baked custard and sprinkle with the diced apricots. Beat the egg whites in a large bowl until stiffly peaking, then gradually beat in the remaining sugar a teaspoonful at a time until thick and glossy (see page 10). Spoon over the jelly, then swirl with the back of the spoon.

Put the dish back in the oven for 15–20 minutes until the meringue is golden and cooked through. Serve warm with cream.

For Monmouth pudding, warm the milk as above, adding ¼ teaspoon grated nutmeg instead of the fruit zests. Add the butter and bread crumbs as above with ½ cup superfine sugar. After the mixture has been left to stand, stir in the egg yolks. Beat the whites (but do not add any more sugar) and fold into the milk mixture. Spoon 4 tablespoons strawberry or raspberry jelly into the base of the pie dish, pour the milk mixture over the top, and bake as above for 30–35 minutes until set and golden. Serve with extra jelly.

steamed pudding with mango

Serves **6**

Preparation time **20 minutes**, plus standing

Cooking time **1 hour 40 minutes**

1 medium **mango**, cut into chunks

2 tablespoons **ready-made** or **homemade vanilla syrup** (see below), plus extra for serving

½ cup **unsalted butter**, softened

½ cup **superfine sugar**

1 teaspoon **vanilla extract**

2 **eggs**

1½ cups **self-rising flour**

4 tablespoons **unsweetened shredded coconut**

1 tablespoon **milk**

Grease a 5 cup pudding basin and line the bottom with a circle of nonstick parchment paper. Arrange the mango chunks in the prepared bowl and drizzle with the vanilla syrup.

Put the butter, sugar, vanilla extract, eggs, and flour in a bowl and beat for 1–2 minutes until creamy. Stir in the coconut and milk, then spoon the mixture into the pudding basin. Level the surface.

Cover the bowl with a double thickness of pleated nonstick parchment paper and secure under the rim with string. Cover with foil, tucking the edges firmly under the rim.

Put the bowl in a steamer or large pan. Half-fill the pan with boiling water and cover with a tight-fitting lid. Steam gently for 1 hour 40 minutes, topping up the water as necessary, then allow to stand for 10 minutes.

Invert the pudding onto a serving plate and drizzle with extra vanilla syrup.

For vanilla syrup, put ⅔ cup superfine sugar in a small heavy pan with ½ cup water, and heat gently until the sugar dissolves. Boil for 6–8 minutes until the syrup is golden. Immediately dip the bottom of the pan into cold water to stop cooking. Add ½ cup hot water and 2 vanilla beans slit along their length (and, if desired, a cinnamon stick or a few whole cloves). Reheat to mix in the extra water. Leave until cooled, then pour into a clean bottle. Seal and shake the bottle to bring out the vanilla flavor. Store for several days and shake before use.

steamed apple pudding

Serves **4**
Preparation time **20 minutes**
Cooking time **2 hours**

½ cup **unsalted butter**
4 tablespoons **corn syrup**
2 **cooking apples**, about
   1 lb in total, cored and
   peeled
7 tablespoons **superfine
   sugar**
2 **eggs**, beaten
1¾ cups **self-rising flour**
grated zest of 1 **orange** and
   3 tablespoons of the juice

Grease the inside of a 5 cup pudding basin lightly and line the base with a small circle of nonstick parchment paper. Spoon in the syrup, then thickly slice 1 apple and arrange in an even layer on top. Coarsely grate the remaining apple.

Cream the butter and sugar in a bowl until pale and creamy. Gradually mix in alternate spoonfuls of beaten egg and flour until both have all been added and the mixture is smooth.

Stir in the grated apple, orange zest, and juice, then spoon into the pudding basin. Level the surface and cover with a piece of pleated nonstick parchment paper and foil. Tie in place with string, adding a string handle.

Lower the basin into the top of a steamer set over a saucepan of simmering water, cover with a lid, and steam for 2 hours until the pudding is well risen and a knife comes out cleanly when inserted into the center of the pudding.

Remove the foil and paper, loosen the edge of the pudding, and turn out onto a plate with a rim. Serve immediately with custard or ice cream.

For cranberry & orange steamed pudding, cook 1¼ cups frozen cranberries in a saucepan with the juice of 1 orange for 5 minutes until softened. Spoon 2 tablespoons raspberry jelly into the prepared pudding basin, then add the cranberries. Make the pudding as above using 1 peeled, cored, and grated cooking apple, also adding the grated zest of 1 orange. Cover and steam as above.

double chocolate puddings

Serves **6**
Preparation time **25 minutes**
Cooking time **18–20 minutes**

½ cup **unsalted butter**, at
   room temperature, or
   soft margarine
½ cup **light brown sugar**
1 cup **self-rising flour**
2 tablespoons **cocoa powder**
2 **eggs**
3 oz or 3 squares **bittersweet
   chocolate**
3½ oz **white chocolate**,
   broken into pieces
⅔ cup **heavy cream**
¼ teaspoon **vanilla extract**

Put the butter or margarine, sugar, flour, cocoa, and eggs into a mixing bowl or food processor and beat together until smooth. Divide the mixture between 6 greased sections of a deep muffin pan, then press ½ square of dark chocolate into each and cover with the pudding mixture.

Bake in a preheated oven, 350°F, for 18–20 minutes until well risen, slightly crusty around the edges, and the center springs back when pressed with a fingertip.

Meanwhile, warm the white chocolate, cream, and vanilla extract together in a small saucepan, stirring until the chocolate has completely melted.

Loosen the edges of the baked puddings with a round-bladed knife, then turn out and transfer to shallow serving bowls. Drizzle with the white chocolate cream and serve immediately.

For walnut & chocolate puddings, omit the cocoa powder from the puddings and mix the butter, sugar, and eggs with 1 cup self-rising flour, ⅓ cup roughly chopped walnuts, and 2 level teaspoons instant coffee dissolved in 3 teaspoons boiling water. Spoon into the muffin pan and press the chocolate into the center of each one as above. Bake as above and serve with pouring cream.

rice pudding with drunken raisins

Serves **4**
Preparation time **10 minutes**,
  plus soaking
Cooking time **2 hours**

⅓ cup **raisins**
2 tablespoons **fortified wine**
  (such as **Pedro Ximénez**,
  Madeira, or **sweet sherry**)
2 tablespoons **unsalted
  butter**, diced
⅔ cup **pudding rice**
2 tablespoons **superfine
  sugar**
2½ cups **milk**
large pinch of grated **nutmeg**
  and **cinnamon**

Put the raisins in a small saucepan with the fortified wine and warm together, or microwave the raisins and wine in a small bowl for 30 seconds on full power. Allow to soak for 30 minutes or longer if time allows.

Grease a 4 cup pie dish, then put in the rice and the sugar. Spoon the raisins on top, then cover with the milk. Dot with the butter and sprinkle with the spices.

Cook in a preheated oven, 300°F, for 2 hours until the pudding is golden on top, the rice is tender, and the milk thick and creamy. Spoon into bowls and serve with spoonfuls of extra-thick cream.

For traditional rice pudding, omit the raisins and fortified wine and add the rice and sugar to the greased pie dish. Pour over 1¾ cups milk and ⅔ cup heavy cream. Dot with butter as above, then sprinkle with just-grated nutmeg. Bake, then serve with spoonfuls of strawberry jelly.

chocolate & marshmallow torte

Serves **8**
Preparation time **40 minutes**,
  plus cooling
Cooking time **25–30 minutes**

7 oz **bittersweet chocolate**,
  broken into pieces
½ cup **unsalted butter**
5 **eggs**, separated
¾ cup **superfine sugar**
2 tablespoons **all-purpose
  flour**, sifted
½ teaspoon **ground cinnamon**
2 tablespoons **warm water**
1¼ cups **heavy cream**
2 cups **mini pink
  and white marshmallows**

Put the chocolate and butter in a bowl set over a saucepan of gently simmering water and allow to melt.

Beat the egg whites in a large bowl until stiff, moist-looking peaks are formed, then gradually beat in half the sugar, a teaspoonful at a time, until thick and glossy (see page 10). Using the still dirty whisk, beat the egg yolks and remaining sugar in a third bowl until very thick.

Mix the warm chocolate and butter mixture gradually into the egg yolks. Stir in the flour and cinnamon, then loosen the mixture with the measured warm water. Gently fold in a spoonful of the meringue, then fold in the remainder.

Pour the mixture into a greased and base-lined 9 inch springform pan. Bake in a preheated oven, 350°F, for 25–30 minutes until well risen and the top is crusty and the center only just set. Allow to cool for 2 hours in the pan.

Remove the torte from the pan, discarding the lining paper. Cut into wedges. Softly whip the cream, then top wedges of torte with spoonfuls of cream and a sprinkling of marshmallows.

For mixed nut torte, fold in ⅔ cup mixed pistachios, hazelnuts, and almonds, roughly chopped, after the flour and cinnamon. Serve with 4 tablespoons toasted slivered almonds instead of the marshmallows.

topsy-turvy banana gingercake

Serves **6**
Preparation time **25 minutes**
Cooking time **30 minutes**

4 tablespoons **corn syrup**,
   plus extra to serve
4 tablespoons **light brown
   sugar**
3 large **bananas**, halved
   lengthwise
juice of **1 lemon**

Gingercake
½ cup **unsalted butter**
½ cup **light brown sugar**
¼ cup **corn syrup**, plus extra
   for drizzling
2 **eggs**
4 tablespoons **milk**
1 cup **wholewheat
   all-purpose flour**
1 teaspoon **baking soda**
2 teaspoons **ground ginger**

Grease a roasting pan with a base measurement of 9 x 7 inches and line the base with nonstick parchment paper. Spoon the syrup and sugar into the base. Toss the bananas in the lemon juice, then arrange cut side downwards in the pan.

Heat the butter, sugar, and syrup for the gingercake gently in a medium saucepan, stirring until melted. Take the pan off the heat.

Beat the eggs and milk in a pitcher, then mix the flour, baking soda, and ginger in a bowl. Gradually stir the milk mixture into the pan of melted butter, then stir in the flour mix and beat until smooth.

Pour the mixture over the bananas, then bake them in a preheated oven, 350°F, for 30 minutes until well risen and the center springs back when pressed.

Allow to cool for 5 minutes, then loosen the edge and invert the pan onto a large plate with a rim. Remove the pan and lining paper, then cut the pudding into portions. Serve drizzled with a little extra syrup or custard.

For homemade custard, to serve with the gingercake, beat 3 egg yolks with 3 tablespoons superfine sugar and a few drops vanilla extract in a bowl. In a pan bring 1¼ cups milk just to a boil, then gradually mix into the yolks. Return to the pan. Heat gently, stirring continuously until the custard thickens and coats the back of the spoon (don't boil or the custard will curdle). If making in advance, sprinkle the surface with a little extra sugar to stop a skin forming.

pear & hazelnut squares

Serves **6**

Preparation time **25 minutes**

Cooking time **25 minutes**

½ cup **unsalted butter**, at
  room temperature, or
  soft margarine

½ cup **superfine sugar**

1 cup **self-rising flour**

2 **eggs**

1 teaspoon **ground cinnamon**

½ cup **hazelnuts**, roughly
  chopped

3 **pears**, quartered, cored,
  and peeled and each piece
  halved again

confectioners' sugar, for
  dusting

Blackberry sauce

1½ cups **blackberries**

2 tablespoons **superfine
  sugar**

4 tablespoons **water**

Beat the butter or margarine, sugar, flour, eggs, and
cinnamon together in a bowl or combine in a food
processor until smooth. Stir in two-thirds of the
hazelnuts. Grease a roasting pan with a base
measurement of 9 x 7 inches and line the base with
nonstick parchment paper. Spoon the mixture into the
pan and smooth into an even layer.

Arrange the pears randomly over the pudding mix,
then sprinkle with the remaining hazelnuts. Bake in
a preheated oven, 350°F, for 25 minutes until golden
brown and the cake is well risen and springs back
when pressed in the center.

Cook 1 cup of the blackberries in a saucepan with the
sugar and water for 5 minutes until soft, then puree
until smooth. Cut the cake into portions, dust with
sifted confectioners' sugar, and serve drizzled with the
warm sauce, with the remaining blackberries.

For apple squares with chocolate sauce, omit the
cinnamon and hazelnuts from the pudding mix, adding
the grated zest of ½ orange instead. Spoon into the
pan, then top with 3 cored, peeled, and thickly sliced
dessert apples and bake as above. Heat 4 tablespoons
chocolate and hazelnut spread in a saucepan with
6 tablespoons milk to make a smooth chocolate
sauce. Cut the cake into squares, dust with sifted
confectioners' sugar, and serve hot with the sauce.

apricot clafouti

Serves **4**
Preparation time **15 minutes**,
   plus standing
Cooking time **25 minutes**

½ cup **all-purpose flour**
2 tablespoons **superfine
   sugar**
grated zest of ½ **lemon**
3 tablespoons **unsalted
   butter**
1 **egg**
1 **egg yolk**
few drops **vanilla extract**
⅔ cup mixed **milk** and **water**
13½ oz can **apricot halves**,
   drained
confectioners' sugar, for
   dusting

Sift the flour into a bowl and add the sugar and lemon zest. Melt 2 tablespoons of the butter, then add to the flour with the whole egg, egg yolk, and vanilla extract. Gradually beat in the milk and water until smooth. Allow to stand for 30 minutes or longer.

Grease liberally 4 individual ¾ cup metal pudding molds with the remaining butter. Quarter the apricots and divide among the molds. Stand the molds on a baking sheet, then cook in a preheated oven, 375°F, for 5 minutes.

Pour the batter quickly into the pudding molds so that the mix sizzles in the hot butter. Bake for about 20 minutes until well risen and golden brown. Dust the tops with sifted confectioners' sugar and serve immediately, as the puddings sink as they cool.

For cherry clafouti, make the batter with the grated zest of ½ orange instead of the lemon. Drain an 11 oz jar of morello cherries in syrup and divide the cherries between the pudding molds as above. Bake the fruit and then add the batter as above.

orchard fruit crumble

Serves **6**
Preparation time **20 minutes**
Cooking time **30–35 minutes**

2 **dessert apples**
2 **pears**
13 oz **red plums**, quartered
   and pitted
2 tablespoons **water**
⅓ cup **superfine sugar**
1 cup **all-purpose flour**
¼ cup **unsalted butter**, diced
¾ cup **shredded coconut**
¼ cup **milk chocolate chips**

Quarter, core, and peel the apples and pears. Slice the quarters and add the slices to a 5 cup pie dish. Add the plums and the water, then sprinkle with 2 tablespoons of the sugar. Cover the dish with foil and bake in a preheated oven, 350°F, for 10 minutes.

Put the remaining sugar in a bowl with the flour and butter, then blend the butter in with your fingertips or an electric mixer until the mixture resembles fine crumbs. Stir in the coconut and chocolate chips.

Remove the foil from the fruit and spoon the crumble over the top. Bake for 20–25 minutes until golden brown and the fruit is tender. Serve warm with custard or cream.

For plum & orange crumble, put 1½ lb plums, quartered and pitted, into a 5 cup pie dish with ¼ cup superfine sugar. Make the crumble as above, adding the grated zest of 1 small orange and ½ cup ground almonds instead of the coconut and chocolate chips. Bake as above.

red rice risotto & sautéed grapes

Serves **4**

Preparation time **15 minutes**

Cooking time **44–55 minutes**

⅓ cup **unsalted butter**

¾ cup **Camargue red rice**, rinsed with cold water and drained

3–4 cups **milk**

½ teaspoon **ground mixed spice**, plus a little extra to decorate

¼ cup **light brown sugar**

1 ¼ cups **red seedless grapes**, halved

sour cream

Heat two-thirds of the butter in a saucepan, add the rice, and cook gently for 2 minutes, stirring. Heat the milk in a separate saucepan, pour about one-third over the rice and add the spice.

Cook the rice gently for 40–50 minutes, stirring occasionally until the rice is tender and creamy, topping up with ladlefuls of milk as the rice swells and stirring more frequently toward the end of the cooking time.

Take the rice off the heat and stir in the sugar. Heat the remaining butter in a skillet, add the grapes, and fry for 2–3 minutes until hot. Spoon the risotto into shallow bowls, top with spoonfuls of sour cream, then spoon the grapes and a little extra spice on top. Serve immediately.

For cherry risotto, fry ¾ cup white risotto rice in ¼ cup butter, then cook with 2½–3 cups warmed milk as above, omitting the ground spice and adding 1 teaspoon vanilla extract and ⅓ cup dried cherries instead. Simmer gently for 20–25 minutes until the rice is soft and creamy. Stir in ¼ cup superfine sugar. Omit the grapes and top the risotto with spoonfuls of sour cream.

toffee & banana crêpes

Serves **4**

Preparation time **15 minutes**, plus resting

Cooking time **30 minutes**

1 cup **all-purpose flour**

pinch **salt**

1 **egg**

1 **egg yolk**

1 ¼ cups **milk**

2–3 tablespoons **sunflower oil**

2 **bananas**, sliced

Toffee sauce

¼ cup **unsalted butter**

¼ cup **light brown sugar**

2 tablespoons **corn syrup**

⅔ cup **heavy cream**

Sift the flour into a bowl, add the salt, egg, and egg yolk, then gradually beat in the milk to make a smooth batter. Set aside for 30 minutes.

Put the butter, sugar, and syrup for the toffee sauce in a small saucepan and heat gently, stirring occasionally, until the butter has melted and the sugar dissolved. Bring to a boil and cook for 3–4 minutes until just beginning to darken around the edges.

Take the pan off the heat, then gradually pour in the cream. Tilt the pan to mix and as bubbles subside stir with a wooden spoon. Set aside.

Pour the oil for cooking the crêpes into an 7 inch skillet, heat, and then pour off the excess into a small bowl or pitcher. Pour a little batter over the base of the pan, tilt the pan to coat the base evenly with batter, then cook for 2 minutes until the underside is golden. Loosen with a spatula, turn over, and cook the second side in the same way. When cooked, slide onto a plate and keep hot. Cook the remaining batter, oiling the pan as needed.

Fold the crêpes and arrange on serving plates. Top with banana slices and drizzle with the toffee sauce.

For citrus crêpes, make the crêpes as above, then drizzle them with the freshly squeezed juice of 1 lemon and 1 orange. Sprinkle with ¼ cup superfine sugar before serving.

cranberry eve's pudding

Serves **6**

Preparation time **25 minutes**

Cooking time **40–50 minutes**

1½ lb **cooking apples**,
  quartered, cored, peeled,
  and thickly sliced

1 cup **frozen cranberries**

⅓ cup **superfine sugar**

1 tablespoon **water**

confectioners' sugar, for
  dusting

Topping

½ cup **unsalted butter**, at
  room temperature, or
  soft margarine

½ cup **superfine sugar**

1 cup **self-rising flour**

2 **eggs**

grated zest of 1 small **orange**,
  plus 2 tablespoons of the
  juice

Put the apples and cranberries into a 6 cup, 2 inch deep ovenproof dish and sprinkle with the sugar and water. Cook, uncovered, in a preheated oven, 350°F, for 10 minutes.

Put the butter, sugar, flour, and eggs for the topping in a bowl, and beat together until smooth. Stir in the orange zest and juice.

Spoon the mixture over the partially cooked fruit and spread into an even layer. Return to the oven and cook for 30–40 minutes until the topping is golden and the center springs back when pressed with a fingertip. Dust with sifted confectioners' sugar and serve warm with custard or cream.

For apple & blackberry pudding, omit the cranberries and add ¾ cup frozen blackberries. Make the topping as above, but add the grated zest of 1 lemon and 2 tablespoons of the juice instead of the orange zest and juice.

pastries, pies, & tarts

gingered profiteroles

Serves **4**

Preparation time **35 minutes**,
 plus cooling

Cooking time **20 minutes**

⅔ cup **water**

¼ cup **unsalted butter**

pinch **salt**

½ cup **all-purpose flour**, sifted

2 **eggs**

½ teaspoon **vanilla extract**

1 cup **heavy cream**

⅓ cup finely chopped **candied
 ginger**

Sauce

5 oz **bittersweet chocolate**,
 broken into pieces

⅔ cup **milk**

¼ cup **superfine sugar**

2 tablespoons **brandy**

Pour the measured water into a medium saucepan, add the butter and salt, and heat until the butter has melted. Bring up to a boil, then take off the heat and stir in the flour. Put the pan back on the heat and cook briefly, stirring until the mixture makes a smooth ball. Allow to cool.

Beat the eggs and vanilla extract together, then gradually beat into the flour mixture until smooth. Spoon the mixture into a large pastry bag fitted with a ¾ inch plain tip. Lightly grease a large baking sheet then pipe on 20 balls, leaving space between them.

Bake in a preheated oven, 400°F, for 15 minutes until well risen. Make a slit in the side of each ball for the steam to escape, return to the turned-off oven for 5 minutes, then take out and cool.

Make the sauce by heating the chocolate, milk, and sugar in a saucepan and stirring until smooth. Take off the heat and mix in the brandy.

Whip the cream until it forms soft swirls, fold in the ginger, then enlarge the slit in each profiterole and spoon in the ginger cream. Pile into serving dishes and drizzle with reheated sauce.

For Black Forest puffs, drain and chop a 14 oz can of black cherries in juice. Fold into the whipped cream instead of the ginger, then fill the profiteroles as above. Omit the brandy from the sauce, adding 2 tablespoons kirsch instead.

peach & blueberry jalousie

Serves **6**
Preparation time **30 minutes**
Cooking time **20–25 minutes**

1 lb chilled **ready-made puff
pastry** or **homemade flaky
pastry** (see page 15)
a little **flour**, for dusting
4 ripe **peaches** or **nectarines**,
thickly sliced
1 cup **blueberries**
¼ cup **superfine sugar**, plus a
little extra to decorate
grated zest of ½ **lemon**
1 **egg**, beaten
confectioners' sugar, for
dusting

Roll out half the pastry on a lightly floured surface
and trim to a 12 x 7 inch rectangle. Transfer to a lightly
greased baking sheet.

Pile the peach or nectarine slices on top, leaving a
1 inch border of pastry showing, then sprinkle on the
blueberries, sugar, and lemon zest. Brush the pastry
border with a little beaten egg.

Roll out the remaining pastry to a little larger than the
first piece, then trim to 13 x 8 inches. Fold in half
lengthwise, then make cuts in from the fold about
½ inch apart and about 2½ inches long, leaving a wide
uncut border of pastry.

Lift the pastry over the fruit, unfold so that the fruit and
bottom layer of pastry are completely covered, then
press the pastry edges together. Trim if needed. Knock
up the edges with a knife, then flute (see page 14).

Brush the top of the pastry with beaten egg, sprinkle
with a little extra sugar, and bake in a preheated oven,
400°F, for 20–25 minutes until the pastry is well risen
and golden brown. Serve cut into squares, warm or
cold, with cream or ice cream.

For apple & blackberry jalousie, replace the
peaches and blueberries with 4 Granny Smith
apples, cored, quartered, and thickly sliced, and
¾ cup blackberries.

strawberry choux puffs

Makes **12**
Preparation time **30 minutes**
Cooking time **30 minutes**

¼ cup **unsalted butter**, cut
  into pieces
⅔ cup **water**
½ cup **all-purpose flour**, sifted
2 **eggs**, beaten
1 teaspoon **vanilla extract**
2 cups **strawberries**, thinly
  sliced
confectioners' sugar, for
  dusting

Crème pâtissière
1 **vanilla bean**
⅔ cup **milk**
⅔ cup **heavy cream**
4 **egg yolks**
3 tablespoons **superfine
  sugar**
2 tablespoons **all-purpose
  flour**

Grease a large baking sheet lightly and sprinkle with water. Melt the butter in a medium saucepan with the water. Bring to a boil, then remove from the heat.

Add the sifted flour and beat until the mix forms a ball. Allow to cool for 15 minutes, then gradually beat in the eggs until smooth and glossy. Add the vanilla extract.

Place 12 equal spoonfuls of the mix, spaced well apart, on the sheet and bake in a preheated oven, 400°F, for 25 minutes or until well risen and golden. Slit around the middle of each and return to the oven for 3 minutes. Transfer to a rack to cool.

Make the crème pâtissière. Slit the vanilla bean and scrape out the seeds. Put milk and heavy cream in a pan and add the seeds and pod. Bring almost to a boil, then allow to stand for 20 minutes. Beat together the yolks, superfine sugar, and all-purpose flour. Remove the pod, reheat the milk mix, then gradually beat into the yolks. Pour back into the pan and cook gently for 4–5 minutes, stirring until very thick. Turn into a bowl, cover with plastic wrap, and allow to cool.

Open out each puff and divide the sliced strawberries among them. Pile the crème pâtissière on top and push the puffs back together so the strawberries and crème pâtissière still show around the center. Dust with confectioners' sugar before serving.

For lemon & peach buns, whip ⅔ cup heavy cream until it forms soft swirls. Fold in ⅓ cup Greek or whole milk yogurt and 3 tablespoons lemon curd. Fill each puff with 2 thinly sliced ripe peaches and spoonfuls of lemon cream. Dust with confectioners' sugar.

pear dumplings with figs

Serves **6**
Preparation time **40 minutes**
Cooking time **15–20 minutes**

10 ready-to-eat **dried figs**,
  finely chopped
grated zest and juice of
  1 large **orange**
6 firm, ripe **pears**
1 lb chilled **ready-made puff
  pastry** or **homemade flaky
  pastry** (see page 15)
a little **flour**, for dusting
1 **egg**, beaten
confectioners' sugar, for
  dusting

Put the figs in a small saucepan with the orange zest
and juice. Cover and simmer gently for 5 minutes until
soft, adding a little extra water if needed. Allow to cool.

Peel the pears and take out the cores via the bases.
Trim off the bases so that they stand upright, then
spoon the fig mixture into the core cavity and press
down firmly.

Roll the pastry out thinly on a lightly floured surface
and trim to a 17 x 15 inch rectangle. Cut a 2½ inch
wide strip off one of the long sides, then cut the strip
into 6 small squares. Place each square under the base
of a pear to stop the stuffing coming out.

Brush the remaining pastry with beaten egg, then cut
into long thin strips about 1 inch wide. Take the strips
one at a time and wind around each pear, beginning at
the top and curling around the pear, with the strip
slightly overlapping, until the base is reached. Add a
second strip if needed.

Put the dumplings on a greased baking sheet and
cook in a preheated oven, 400°F, for 15–20 minutes
until golden brown. Dust with sifted confectioners'
sugar and serve hot with custard.

For Christmas gingered pear dumplings, combine
3 tablespoons good-quality fruit mincemeat with
2 tablespoons finely chopped candied ginger. Spoon
the mixture into 6 peeled, cored pears. Wrap in pastry
and cook as above. Serve with sour cream mixed with
a little brandy or whiskey.

freeform apple & mixed berry pie

Serves **6**

Preparation time **30 minutes**, plus chilling

Cooking time **20–25 minutes**

2¼ cups **all-purpose flour**, plus extra for dusting

¾ cup **confectioners' sugar**

½ cup **unsalted butter**, at room temperature, diced

2 **eggs**

a little **milk** or beaten **egg**, to glaze

superfine sugar, to decorate

Filling

2 **cooking apples**, about 1 lb, cored, peeled, and thickly sliced

1¼ cups **frozen mixed berries** (no need to defrost)

½ cup **confectioners' sugar**

2 teaspoons **cornstarch**

Put the flour on a large board or straight onto the work surface, add the confectioners' sugar and butter, then make a dip in the center and add the eggs. Begin to mix the eggs and butter together with your fingertips, gradually drawing the flour and sugar into the mix until it begins to clump together and you can squeeze the pastry into a ball. Knead the pastry lightly, then chill in the refrigerator for 15 minutes.

Mix together the apples, frozen mixed berries, confectioners' sugar, and cornstarch for the filling.

Roll out the pastry on a lightly floured surface until it forms a rough-shaped circle about 13 inches in diameter. Lift it over a rolling pin onto a large greased baking sheet. Pile the fruit mix high in the center of the pastry, then bring the edges of the pastry up and around the fruit, shaping into soft pleats and leaving the center of the fruit mound exposed.

Brush the outside of the pie with a little milk or beaten egg and sprinkle with superfine sugar. Bake in a preheated oven, 375°F, for 20–25 minutes until the pastry is golden and the fruit tender. Serve warm or cold with custard or cream.

For spiced plum & peach pie, replace the apples and berries with 13 oz ripe red plums, pitted and sliced, and 2 ripe peaches, sliced. Mix with the sugar and cornstarch as above, adding ½ teaspoon ground cinnamon. Make the pie and bake as above.

portuguese custard tarts

Makes **12**
Preparation time **25 minutes**,
  plus cooling
Cooking time **35 minutes**

1 tablespoon **vanilla sugar**
½ teaspoon **ground cinnamon**
14½ oz chilled **ready-made**
  or **homemade sweet**
  shortcrust pastry (see
  page 15)
a little **flour**, for dusting
3 **eggs**
2 **egg yolks**
2 tablespoons **superfine**
  sugar
1 teaspoon **vanilla extract**
1¼ cups **heavy cream**
⅔ cup **milk**
confectioners' sugar, for
  dusting

Mix the vanilla sugar with the cinnamon. Cut the pastry in half and roll out each piece on a lightly floured surface to an 8 inch square. Sprinkle 1 square with the spiced sugar and position the second square on top. Reroll the pastry to a 16 x 12 inch rectangle and cut out 12 circles, each 4 inches across, using a large cutter or small bowl as a guide.

Press the pastry circles into the sections of a 12-cup nonstick muffin pan, pressing them firmly into the bottom and around the sides. Prick each pastry base, line with a square of foil, add macaroni or pie weights, and bake blind (see page 12) in a preheated oven, 375°F, for 10 minutes. Remove the foil and macaroni or weights and bake for an additional 5 minutes. Reduce the oven temperature to 325°F.

Beat together the eggs, egg yolks, superfine sugar, and vanilla extract. Heat the cream and milk in a pan until bubbling around the edges and pour it over the egg mixture, stirring. Strain the custard into a pitcher and pour into the pastry shells.

Bake for about 20 minutes or until the custard is only just set. Let the tarts cool in the pan, then remove and serve dusted with confectioners' sugar.

For French prune custard tarts, put a ready-to-eat pitted prune in the base of each blind-baked pastry shell, then pour the custard over and bake as above. Serve warm with spoonfuls of sour cream.

lemon meringue pie

Serves **6**
Preparation time **40 minutes**, plus chilling and standing
Cooking time **35–40 minutes**

12 oz chilled **ready-made or homemade sweet shortcrust pastry** (see page 15)
a little **flour**, for dusting
1 cup **superfine sugar**
¼ cup **cornstarch**
grated zest and juice of **2 lemons**
4 **eggs**, separated
¾–1 cup **water**

Roll out the pastry thinly on a lightly floured surface and use to line an 8 inch diameter x 2 inch deep removable-bottomed fluted tart pan, pressing evenly into the sides (see page 11). Trim the top and prick the base. Chill for 15 minutes, then line with nonstick parchment paper, add macaroni or pie weights, and bake blind (see page 12) in a preheated oven, 375°F, for 15 minutes. Remove the paper and macaroni or weights and bake for 5 more minutes.

Put ⅓ cup of the sugar in a bowl with the cornstarch and lemon zest, add the egg yolks, and mix smooth. Make the lemon juice up to 1¼ cups with water, pour into a saucepan, and bring to a boil. Gradually mix into the yolk mixture, beating until smooth. Pour back into the pan and bring to a boil, beating until very thick. Pour into the pastry shell and spread level.

Beat the egg whites until they form stiff peaks. Gradually beat in the remaining sugar, a teaspoonful at a time, then beat for 1–2 minutes more until thick and glossy (see page 10). Spoon over the lemon layer to cover completely and swirl with a spoon.

Reduce the oven to 350°F and cook the meringue for 15–20 minutes until it is golden and cooked through. Allow to stand for 15 minutes, then remove the tart pan and transfer to a serving plate. Serve warm or cold with cream.

For citrus meringue pie, mix the grated zest of 1 lime, 1 lemon, and ½ small orange with the cornstarch. Squeeze the juice from the fruits and make up to 1¼ cups with water. Continue as above.

74

classic lemon tart

Serves **8**

Preparation time **20 minutes**,
plus chilling and cooling

Cooking time **45–50 minutes**

14½ oz chilled **ready-made**
or **homemade sweet
shortcrust pastry** (see
page 15)

3 **eggs**

1 **egg yolk**

1¾ cups **heavy cream**

½ cup **superfine sugar**

⅔ cup **lemon juice**

confectioners' sugar, for
dusting

Roll out pastry thinly on a lightly floured surface and use it to line a 10 inch fluted tart pan (see page 11). Prick the pastry shell with a fork and then chill for 15 minutes.

Line the pastry shell with nonstick parchment paper, add macaroni or pie weights, and bake blind (see page 12) in a preheated oven, 375°F, for 15 minutes. Remove the paper and macaroni or weights and bake for 10 minutes more until crisp and golden. Remove from the oven and reduce the temperature to 300°F.

Beat together the eggs, egg yolk, heavy cream, sugar, and lemon juice, then pour into the pastry shell.

Bake for 20–25 minutes or until the filling is just set. Let the tart cool completely, then dust with confectioners' sugar and serve.

For mixed berries with cassis, to serve with the tart, halve or slice 1½ cups strawberries, depending on their size, and mix with 1 cup raspberries, 1 cup blueberries, 3 tablespoons superfine sugar, and 2 tablespoons crème de cassis. Soak for 1 hour before serving.

gateau pithiviers with plums

Serves **6**
Preparation time **30 minutes**
Cooking time **25–30 minutes**

½ cup **unsalted butter**, at
room temperature
½ cup **superfine sugar**
1 cup **ground almonds**
few drops **almond essence**
1 **egg**, beaten, plus extra for
glazing
1 lb chilled **ready-made puff
pastry** or **homemade flaky
pastry** (see page 15)
a little **flour**, for dusting
12 oz **plums**, pitted and
thickly sliced
confectioners' sugar, for
dusting

Cream the butter and sugar together in a bowl
until pale and smooth. Add the almonds and almond
extract, then the egg, and mix together until smooth.

Roll out half the pastry thinly on a lightly floured
surface and trim to a 10 inch circle using a dinner plate
as a guide. Place on a wetted baking sheet, then
spread the almond paste over the top leaving a 1 inch
border of pastry around the edges. Arrange the plums
in a single layer on top. Brush the pastry border with a
little beaten egg.

Roll out the remaining pastry thinly and trim to a circle
a little larger than the first. Cut 5 or 6 swirly "S" shapes
out of the center of the pastry, then lift over a rolling
pin and position on the almond paste. Press the edges
together to seal and trim to neaten if needed. Knock
up the edge to separate the pastry layers slightly, then
flute the edge (see page 14).

Brush the top with beaten egg and bake in a
preheated oven, 400°F, for 25–30 minutes until well
risen and golden.

Allow to cool slightly, then dust the top with
confectioners' sugar and serve cut into wedges
with cream.

For brandied prune Pithiviers, soak 1 cup ready-to-
eat pitted prunes in 3 tablespoons brandy, then
arrange over the almond paste instead of the plums.
Continue as above.

pecan, maple syrup, & choc tart

Serves **8**

Preparation time **20 minutes**,
plus chilling and cooling

Cooking time **1 hour–1 hour
10 minutes**

1½ cups **all-purpose flour**,
sifted, plus extra for dusting

¼ cup **cocoa powder**, sifted

¼ teaspoon **salt**

½ cup chilled **unsalted butter**,
diced

1 **egg**, lightly beaten

2–3 teaspoons **cold water**

Filling

½ cup **unsalted butter**,
softened

½ cup **light brown sugar**

2 **eggs**, beaten

4 tablespoons **all-purpose
flour**

pinch **salt**

¾ cup **maple syrup**

1½ cups **pecan nuts**, toasted

⅔ cup **pine nuts**, lightly
toasted

2 oz **bittersweet chocolate**,
chopped

Place the flour, cocoa powder, and salt in a bowl,
add the butter and blend in with the fingertips until the
mixture resembles fine bread crumbs. Add the egg and
water and continue mixing until the pastry just starts to
come together. Transfer to a lightly floured surface,
knead gently, and form into a flat disk. Wrap the dough
in plastic wrap and chill for 30 minutes.

Roll out the dough thinly on a lightly floured surface
and use it to line a 9 inch square tart pan (see
page 11). Prick the base and chill for 20 minutes. Line
the pan with nonstick parchment paper, add macaroni
or pie weights, and bake blind (see page 12) in a
preheated oven, 375°F, for 15 minutes. Remove
the paper and weights or macaroni and bake for an
additional 5–10 minutes or until crisp and golden.
Allow to cool. Reduce the temperature to 350°F.

Cream the butter and sugar until pale and light, then
gradually beat in the eggs, adding the flour and salt as
you go until evenly combined. Stir in the syrup (the
mixture may appear to curdle at this stage), nuts, and
chocolate and spoon the mixture into the pastry shell.

Bake for 40–45 minutes until golden and just firm in
the center. Remove from the oven and allow to cool.
Serve warm with heavy cream.

For traditional pecan pie, replace the cocoa with
an extra ¼ cup all-purpose flour and a large pinch of
ground mixed spice in the pastry. Use 2 cups pecan
nuts and omit the pine nuts and chocolate, flavoring
with 1 teaspoon vanilla extract instead.

cherry frangipane tart

Serves **8**

Preparation time **35 minutes**,
 plus chilling and cooling

Cooking time **50 minutes**

14½ oz chilled **ready-made
 or homemade sweet
 shortcrust pastry** (see
 page 15)
a little **flour**, for dusting
1 cup **fresh cherries**, pitted,
 or a 14 oz can, drained
3 eggs
½ cup **superfine sugar**
⅓ cup **unsalted butter**, melted
few drops **almond extract**
1 cup **ground almonds**
2 tablespoons **slivered
 almonds**
confectioners' sugar, for
 dusting

Roll out the pastry on a lightly floured surface until large enough to line a 10 inch greased deep-fluted, removable-bottomed tart pan (see page 11). Lift the pastry over a rolling pin, then press it over the base and sides of the pan. Trim the top, then chill for 15 minutes.

Prick the base of the tart with a fork. Line the pastry with nonstick parchment paper, add macaroni or pie weights, and bake blind (see page 12) in a preheated oven, 375°F, for 15 minutes. Remove the paper and macaroni or weights and cook for an extra 5 minutes.

Arrange the cherries in the base of the tart. Beat the eggs and sugar together until thick and the whisk leaves a trail when lifted out of the mixture. Gently fold in the melted butter and almond extract, then the ground almonds. Pour the mixture over the cherries and sprinkle with the slivered almonds.

Reduce the oven to 350°F, and cook the tart for 30 minutes until golden brown and the filling is set. Check after 20 minutes and cover the top loosely with foil if the tart appears to be browning too quickly.

Allow to cool in the pan for 30 minutes, then remove and dust with sifted confectioners' sugar before serving.

For Bakewell tart, make the tart shell and bake blind as above, then spread 4 tablespoons strawberry or raspberry jelly over the base. Add the almond mixture and slivered almonds and bake as above.

pear & almond tart

Serves **8**

Preparation time **20 minutes**,
plus chilling

Cooking time **50–55 minutes**

14½ oz chilled **ready-made**
   or **homemade sweet**
   shortcrust pastry (see
   page 15)
a little **flour**, for dusting
½ cup **unsalted butter**,
   softened
½ cup **superfine sugar**
1 cup **ground almonds**
2 **eggs**, lightly beaten
1 tablespoon **lemon juice**
3 ripe **pears**, peeled, cored,
   and thickly sliced
¼ cup **slivered almonds**
confectioners' sugar, for
   dusting

Roll out the pastry on a lightly floured surface and use
it to line a 10 inch tart pan (see page 11). Prick the
base with a fork and chill for 30 minutes. Line with
nonstick parchment paper, add macaroni or pie
weights, and bake blind (see page 12) in a preheated
oven, 375°F, for 15 minutes. Remove the parchment
paper and macaroni or weights, and bake for an
additional 5–10 minutes until the pastry is crisp
and golden. Allow to cool completely. Reduce the
temperature to 375°F.

Beat the butter, sugar, and ground almonds together
until smooth, then beat in the eggs and lemon juice.

Arrange the pear slices over the pastry shell and
carefully spread over the almond mixture. Sprinkle with
the slivered almonds and bake for 30 minutes until the
topping is golden and firm to the touch. Remove from
the oven and allow to cool.

Dust the tart with sifted confectioners' sugar and serve
in wedges with chocolate sauce (see below) and some
vanilla ice cream.

For chocolate sauce, to serve as an accompaniment,
melt together 4 oz bittersweet chocolate, chopped,
¼ cup unsalted butter, diced, and 1 tablespoon corn
syrup. Allow to cool slightly.

sweet fruity pizzas

Serves **4**

Preparation time **25 minutes**, plus rising

Cooking time **12–15 minutes**

2 cups **bread flour**, plus extra for dusting

¼ teaspoon **salt**

2 tablespoons **superfine sugar**

¾ teaspoon **active dry yeast**

2 tablespoons **olive oil**

⅔ cup warm **water**

Topping

⅔ cup **full-fat mascarpone cheese**

2 tablespoons **confectioners' sugar**

½ teaspoon **vanilla extract**

2 **peaches**, pitted and sliced

2 **figs**, quartered

1 cup **fresh raspberries**

2 tablespoons **maple syrup**, plus extra to serve

Put the flour, salt, sugar, and yeast in a bowl and mix together. Add the oil, then gradually stir in the measured warm water and mix to a smooth dough. Knead on a lightly floured surface for 5 minutes until smooth and elastic. Put back in the bowl, cover with greased plastic wrap, and leave in a warm place for about 45 minutes until doubled in size.

Knead the dough for a second time, then roll out to 4 rough-shaped circles about 7 inches in diameter. Place on 2 greased baking sheets.

Mix the mascarpone with the confectioners' sugar and vanilla extract, then spread over the pizzas leaving a rim of dough. Arrange the fruit on top. Allow to rise for 15 minutes. Drizzle with maple syrup, then bake in a preheated oven, 400°F, for 12–15 minutes until the pizzas are golden and the bread bases cooked through.

Let stand for 5 minutes, drizzle with a little extra maple syrup, then serve.

For marzipan & nectarine fruit kuchen, add the grated zest of 1 lemon when mixing the bread dough, knead, allow to rise, and knead again as above, then press into a 10 inch greased fluted, removable-bottomed tart pan. Sprinkle with ⅓ cup grated marzipan, then arrange 2 sliced nectarines over the top. Drizzle with 2 tablespoons melted butter and 2 tablespoons superfine sugar. Allow to rise, then bake for 25–30 minutes at the temperature given above, covering with foil after 15 minutes if overbrowning.

mixed berry tartlets

Serves **6**

Preparation time **20 minutes**,
   plus chilling

Cooking time **40–48 minutes**

14½ oz chilled **ready-made**
   or **homemade sweet**
   shortcrust pastry (see
   page 15)
a little **flour**, for dusting
confectioners' sugar, for
   dusting

Filling
½ cup **unsalted butter**,
   softened
½ cup **superfine sugar**
2 **eggs**, lightly beaten
1 cup **ground hazelnuts**
1½ cups **mixed summer**
   berries (such as **raspberries**
   and **blueberries**)

Apricot glaze
¾ cup **apricot jelly**
2 teaspoons **lemon juice**
2 teaspoons **water**

Divide the pastry into 3 pieces and roll each one out
thinly on a lightly floured surface. Use to line 3 small
(5 inch) fluted tart pans (see page 11). Prick the bases
with a fork and chill for 30 minutes. Line with nonstick
parchment paper, add macaroni or pie weights, and
bake blind (see page 12) in a preheated oven, 375°F,
for 10 minutes. Remove the paper and macaroni or
weights, and bake for 5–8 minutes more until the
pastry is crisp and golden. Allow to cool. Reduce the
temperature to 350°F.

Beat the butter and sugar until pale and light, then
gradually beat in the eggs. Fold in the hazelnuts.

Divide the berries among the pastry shells and spoon
over the hazelnut mixture, spreading it flat. Bake for
25–30 minutes or until risen and firm to the touch.

Put the jelly in a small pan with the lemon juice and
measured water and heat gently until the jelly melts.
Increase the heat and boil for 1 minute, remove from
the heat, and press through a fine sieve. Keep warm.

Brush the warm apricot glaze over the tarts as soon
as they come out of the oven. Allow to cool in the pans
and serve dusted with confectioners' sugar.

For raspberry & almondine tart, line an 8 inch tart
pan with pastry and bake blind as above. Sprinkle
with 1¾ cups fresh raspberries. Cream the butter and
sugar as above, then beat in the eggs, 1 cup ground
almonds, and a few drops almond extract. Spoon into
the case and sprinkle with 3 tablespoons slivered
almonds. Bake as above for 35–45 minutes.

deep dish puff apple pie

Serves **6**

Preparation time **40 minutes**, plus chilling

Cooking time **20–25 minutes**

2 lb or about 5 **cooking apples**, quartered, cored, peeled, and thickly sliced

½ cup **superfine sugar**, plus extra for sprinkling

grated zest of 1 small **orange**

½ teaspoon **ground mixed spice** or **ground cinnamon**

3 whole **cloves**

13 oz chilled **ready-made puff pastry** or **homemade flaky pastry** (see page 15)

a little **flour**, for dusting

1 **egg**, beaten

Fill a 5 cup pie dish with the apples. Mix the sugar with the orange zest, mixed spice, and cloves, then sprinkle over the apples.

Roll the pastry out on a lightly floured surface until a little larger than the top of the dish. Cut 2 long strips from the edges, about ½ inch wide. Brush the dish rim with a little beaten egg, press the strips on top, then brush these with egg (see pages 13–14). Lift the remaining pastry over the dish and press the edges together well.

Trim off the excess pastry, knock up the edges with a small knife, then flute. Reroll the trimmings and cut out small heart shapes or circles with a small cookie cutter. Brush the top of the pie with beaten egg, add pastry shapes, then brush these with egg. Sprinkle with a little extra sugar.

Bake in a preheated oven, 400°F, for 20–25 minutes until the pastry is well risen and golden. Serve warm with spoonfuls of crème fraîche or extra-thick cream.

For spiced plum & pear pie, substitute 1 lb sliced pears and 1 lb sliced plums for the apples, sprinkle with ⅓ cup superfine sugar, and add 2 halved star anise, 3 cloves, and ¼ teaspoon ground cinnamon. Omit the fruit zest, then cover with the pastry and continue as above.

mango & palm sugar tatin

Serves **8**

Preparation time **40 minutes**, plus freezing

Cooking time **20–25 minutes**

⅓ cup **unsalted butter**

⅓ cup **palm sugar**, grated, or **light brown sugar**

½ teaspoon ground **mixed spice**

3 small **mangoes**, peeled, pitted, and thickly sliced

12 oz chilled **ready-made puff pastry** or **homemade flaky pastry** (see page 15)

a little **flour**, for dusting

Make the topping. Heat the butter, sugar, and spice together in a 9 inch ovenproof skillet until the butter has melted. Remove the pan from the heat. Carefully arrange the mango slices in the pan, fanning them from the center outward, to make 2 layers.

Roll out the pastry on a lightly floured surface and trim to a round a little larger than the size of the pan. Press it down over the mangoes and into the edges of the pan and pierce a small hole in the center. Bake in a preheated oven, 425°F, for 20–25 minutes until the pastry is risen and golden. Allow to stand for 10 minutes before turning out onto a large plate. Serve with ice cream.

For coconut ice cream, to accompany the tatin, bring 1¼ cups whole milk, 1¾ cups full-fat coconut milk, and 2 star anise just to a boil in a saucepan. Take off the heat, allow to infuse for 20 minutes, then strain. Beat 5 egg yolks with ⅓ cup superfine sugar until pale and creamy. Stir in the cream mix, then pour back into the pan and heat gently, stirring until it coats the back of the spoon. Cool, then freeze in an electric ice-cream machine until thick or in a plastic box in the freezer, beating several times until firm.

pumpkin pie

Serves **6**
Preparation time **30 minutes**
Cooking time **60–75 minutes**

1 lb **pumpkin** or **butternut squash**, weighed after seeding and peeling
3 **eggs**
½ cup **light brown sugar**
2 tablespoons **all-purpose flour**
½ teaspoon **ground cinnamon**
½ teaspoon **ground ginger**
¼ teaspoon **grated nutmeg**
¾ cup **milk**, plus extra for glazing
14½ oz chilled **ready-made** or **homemade sweet shortcrust pastry** (see page 15)
a little **flour**, for dusting
confectioners' sugar, for dusting

Cut the pumpkin or butternut squash into cubes and cook in a covered steamer for 15–20 minutes, until tender. Cool, then puree in a blender or food processor.

Beat the eggs, sugar, flour, and spices together in a bowl until just mixed. Add the pumpkin puree, beat together, then gradually mix in the milk. Set aside.

Roll out three-quarters of the pastry on a lightly floured surface until large enough to line a greased 9 inch x 1 inch deep enamel pie dish. Lift the pastry over the rolling pin and press over the base and sides of the dish. Trim off the excess around the rim and add the trimmings to the reserved pastry. Roll out thinly and cut out decorative leaves, marking the veins. Brush the rim of the pastry in the dish, then press on the leaves, reserving a few. Stand the dish on a baking sheet.

Pour the pumpkin filling into the dish, add a few leaves if desired on top of the filling, then brush these and the dish edges lightly with milk. Bake in a preheated oven, 375°F, for 45–55 minutes until the filling is set and the pastry cooked through. Cover with foil after 20 minutes to stop the pastry edge from overbrowning.

Serve dusted with a little confectioners' sugar, with whipped cream sprinkled with a little extra ground spice, if desired.

For gingered pumpkin pie with maple syrup, omit the brown sugar and add 6 tablespoons maple syrup. Omit the ground cinnamon and nutmeg and increase the ground ginger to 1½ teaspoons, adding 2 tablespoons finely chopped candied or stem ginger.

kaffir lime tart

Serves **8**

Preparation time **20 minutes**, plus chilling

Cooking time **33–40 minutes**

13 oz chilled **ready-made or homemade sweet shortcrust pastry** (see page 15)

a little **flour**, for dusting

¾ cup **superfine sugar**

¾ cup freshly squeezed **lime juice** (4–6 limes)

8 **kaffir lime leaves** or the grated zest of 3 **limes**

3 **eggs**

2 **egg yolks**

¾ cup **unsalted butter**, softened

confectioners' sugar, for dusting

Roll out the pastry on a lightly floured surface and use it to line a 9 inch tart pan (see page 11). Prick the base with a fork and chill for 30 minutes. Line with nonstick parchment paper, add macaroni or pie weights, and bake blind (see page 12) in a preheated oven, 400°F, for 15 minutes. Remove the paper and macaroni or weights, and bake for an additional 12–15 minutes until the pastry is crisp and golden. Set aside to cool.

Make the filling. Put the sugar, lime juice, and kaffir lime leaves or lime zest in a saucepan and heat gently to dissolve the sugar. Bring to a boil and simmer for 5 minutes. Allow to cool for 5 minutes, then strain into a clean pan.

Stir in the eggs, egg yolks, and half the butter and heat gently, stirring, for 1 minute or until the sauce coats the back of the spoon. Add the remaining butter and beat constantly until the mixture thickens.

Transfer the lime mixture to the pastry shell and bake as above for 6–8 minutes until set. Allow to cool and serve warm dusted with confectioners' sugar.

For mango & kiwifruit salad, to serve with the tart, peel, pit, and dice 1 large mango, then mix with 3 peeled and sliced kiwifruits, the seeds scooped from 3 passion fruits, and the juice of 1 lime.

plum tripiti

Makes **24**
Preparation time **40 minutes**
Cooking time **10 minutes**

4 oz **feta cheese**, drained and
   coarsely grated
½ cup **ricotta cheese**
¼ cup **superfine sugar**
¼ teaspoon **ground cinnamon**
1 **egg**, beaten
⅓ cup **unsalted butter**
12 sheets chilled **phyllo
   pastry** from a 7 oz package
a little **flour**, for dusting
12 small red **plums**, halved
   and pitted
confectioners' sugar, for
   dusting

Mix the feta, ricotta, sugar, cinnamon, and egg in a
bowl. Melt the butter in a small saucepan.

Unfold the pastry sheets on a lightly floured surface,
then put one in front of you, with a short side facing
you. Cover the remaining sheets with plastic wrap to
prevent them drying out. Brush the pastry sheet with a
little of the melted butter, then cut in half to make two
long strips. Place a spoonful of the cheese mixture a
little up from the bottom left-hand corner of each strip,
then cover with a plum half. Fold the bottom right-hand
corner of one strip diagonally over the plum to cover
the filling and to make a triangle.

Fold the bottom left-hand corner upward to make a
second triangle, then keep folding until the top of the
strip is reached and the filling is enclosed in a triangle
of pastry. Place on a baking sheet and repeat until
24 triangles have been made using all the filling.

Brush the outside of the triangles with the remaining
butter and cook in a preheated oven, 400°F, for about
10 minutes until the pastry is golden and the plum
juices begin to run from the sides. Dust with a little
sifted confectioners' sugar and allow to cool for
15 minutes before serving.

For gingered peach tripiti, make the filling in the
same way but flavor with 2 tablespoons finely
chopped candied or stem ginger instead of ground
cinnamon. Top with 2 ripe peaches, each cut into
12 pieces.

apple & muscatel strudel

Serves **6**
Preparation time **30 minutes**,
  plus soaking
Cooking time **30–35 minutes**

⅔ cup **muscatel raisins**
2 tablespoons **brandy**
1½ lb **dessert apples**,
  quartered, cored, and cut
  into small dice
1½ cups **fresh white bread
  crumbs**
¼ cup **light brown sugar**
grated zest of 1 **lemon**
⅓ cup **pine nuts**, toasted
1 teaspoon **ground
  cinnamon**, plus extra for
  dusting
12 sheets chilled **phyllo
  pastry** from a 7 oz package
a little **flour**, for dusting
¼ cup **unsalted butter**, melted
2 tablespoons **confectioners'
  sugar**, for dusting

Put the raisins in a bowl and cover with the brandy. Set aside to soak for 2 hours.

Put the apples in a bowl and add the bread crumbs, sugar, lemon zest, pine nuts, cinnamon, and the raisins and their juices. Stir well.

Lay 2 sheets of the pastry on a lightly floured work surface, next to each other and overlapping by about 1 inch to form a larger sheet of pastry. Brush with melted butter, then top with the remaining pastry, brushing each layer with a little butter.

Spread the apple mixture over the pastry, leaving a 2 inch border. Fold the long sides over the filling. Brush with butter and roll up from a short side to form a jelly roll.

Transfer the strudel to a baking sheet, brush with the remaining melted butter, and bake in a preheated oven, 400°F, for 30–35 minutes until lightly golden. Combine the sifted confectioners' sugar with a little extra cinnamon and dust the strudel. Serve hot with custard or whipped cream.

For plum & almond strudel, omit the raisins, brandy, and apples and mix 1¼ lb pitted and thickly sliced red plums with the bread crumbs, sugar, lemon zest, ½ cup ground almonds, and 1 teaspoon ground cinnamon. Continue as above.

double chocolate tart

Serves **6–8**
Preparation time **40 minutes**,
  plus chilling and cooling
Cooking time **40 minutes**

13 oz chilled **ready-made**
  or **homemade sweet**
  shortcrust pastry (see
  page 15)
a little **flour**, for dusting
5 oz **bittersweet chocolate**,
  broken into pieces, plus
  2 oz to decorate
5 oz **white chocolate**
½ cup **unsalted butter**
3 **eggs**
1 **egg yolk**
½ cup **superfine sugar**
2 tablespoons **heavy cream**

Roll out the pastry on a lightly floured surface until large enough to line a greased 9½ inch fluted, removable-bottomed tart pan (see page 11). Drape into the pan using a rolling pin. Press in place and trim off the excess. Prick with a fork, then chill for 15 minutes. Line with nonstick parchment paper, add macaroni or pie weights, and bake blind (see page 12) in a preheated oven, 375°F, for 15 minutes. Remove the paper and macaroni or weights and bake for 5 minutes.

Melt the dark and white chocolate in separate bowls over simmering water (see page 11). Add three-quarters of the butter to the dark chocolate and the rest to the white chocolate. Leave until melted.

Beat the eggs, egg yolk, and sugar in a third bowl for 3–4 minutes until doubled in volume (but not so thick as to leave a trail). Fold two-thirds into the dark chocolate mixture, then pour into the cooked tart shell. Fold the cream into the white chocolate to loosen it, then fold in the remaining beaten egg mixture. Spoon over the dark chocolate layer to completely cover.

Reduce the oven to 325°F and cook the tart for 20 minutes until just set with a slight wobble to the center. Cool for at least 1 hour. Pipe double lines of melted dark chocolate and leave for at least 30 minutes before serving.

For dark chocolate tart, melt 10 oz bittersweet chocolate with ½ cup butter. Beat the eggs and sugar as above and fold into the chocolate mixture. Pour into the baked tart shell and bake for 15 minutes as above. Dust with sifted cocoa powder to serve.

mini nectarine & blueberry tarts

Makes **12**
Preparation time **15 minutes**
Cooking time **6–8 minutes**

2 tablespoons **unsalted butter**
2 teaspoons **olive oil**
4 sheets chilled **phyllo pastry**, each 12 x 7 inches or 2½ oz total weight
a little **flour**, for dusting
2 tablespoons **red berry jelly**
juice of ½ **orange**
4 ripe **nectarines**, halved, pitted, and sliced
1¼ cups **blueberries**
confectioners' sugar, for dusting

Heat the butter and oil in a small saucepan until the butter has melted.

Unfold the pastry on a lightly floured surface and separate into sheets. Brush lightly with the butter mixture, then cut into 24 pieces, each 4 x 3½ inches.

Arrange a piece in each of the sections of a deep 12-cup muffin pan, then add a second piece at a slight angle to the first pieces to give a pretty jagged edge to each pastry shell.

Bake in a preheated oven, 350°F, for 6–8 minutes until golden. Meanwhile, warm the jelly and orange juice in a saucepan, then add the nectarines and blueberries and warm through.

Lift the tart shells carefully out of the muffin pan and transfer to a serving dish. Fill the shells with the warm fruits and dust with sifted confectioners' sugar. Serve with cream or ice cream.

For honeyed grape tarts, make up the tart shells as above. In a saucepan, cook 1½ cups ruby seedless grapes, halved, ¾ cup red grape juice, and 1 tablespoon honey for 5 minutes. Lift out the grapes with a draining spoon, then boil the juice until syrupy. Return the grapes to the pan, then allow to cool. Mix 1 cup Greek or whole milk yogurt with 2 tablespoons honey, spoon into the tart shells and top with the cooled syrupy grapes.

white chocolate & raspberry puffs

Serves **6**
Preparation time **20 minutes**,
  plus chilling
Cooking time **15 minutes**

12 oz chilled **ready-made**
  puff pastry or **homemade**
  flaky pastry (see page 15)
a little **flour**, for dusting
¾ cup **heavy cream**
½ **vanilla bean**
7 oz **white chocolate**,
  chopped
1¼ cups **raspberries**
confectioners' sugar, for
  dusting

Roll out the pastry dough on a lightly floured surface until it is a rectangle ⅛ inch thick. Cut into 6 rectangles, each 5 x 3 inches, and put them on a baking sheet. Chill for 30 minutes. Bake in a preheated oven, 400°F, for 15 minutes until the pastry is puffed and golden. Transfer to a cooling rack to cool.

Put the cream and vanilla bean in a saucepan and heat gently until it reaches boiling point. Remove from the heat and scrape the seeds from the vanilla bean into the cream (discard the pod). Immediately stir in the chocolate and continue stirring until it has melted. Cool, chill for 1 hour until firm, then beat until spreadable.

Split the pastries in half crosswise and fill each with white chocolate cream and raspberries. Serve dusted with sifted confectioners' sugar.

For strawberry custard creams, make the pastry rectangles as above, then cool. Whip ⅔ cup heavy cream until it forms soft swirls, then fold in ½ cup ready-made custard. Split and fill the pastries with custard cream and 1½ cups sliced strawberries. Dust the tops with sifted confectioners' sugar before serving.

papaya, lime, & mango tartlets

Makes **20**
Preparation time **35 minutes**
Cooking time **15–20 minutes**

8 oz chilled **ready-made
   or homemade sweet
   shortcrust pastry** (see
   page 15)
a little **flour**, for dusting
thinly grated zest and juice of
   2 large, juicy **limes**
6 tablespoons **heavy cream**
⅔ cup **full-fat condensed
   milk**
2 tablespoons finely diced
   papaya
2 tablespoons finely diced
   mango
lime zest, to decorate

Roll out the pastry on a lightly floured surface to an ⅛ inch thickness, then, using a 2 inch round cookie or pastry cutter, stamp out 20 rounds. Use the pastry rounds to line 20 x 2 inch mini tartlet pans (see page 11). Prick the pastry bases with a fork. Line with nonstick parchment paper, add macaroni or pie weights, and bake blind (see page 12) in a preheated oven, 375°F, for 10 minutes, then remove the paper and macaroni or weights and return the shells to the oven for 5–10 minutes or until they are crisp and golden. Remove from the oven.

Put the lime zest in a blender with the cream and condensed milk and pulse until well combined. With the motor running, slowly pour in the lime juice and process until blended. (Alternatively, mix well by hand.) Transfer to a bowl, cover, and chill in the refrigerator for 3–4 hours or until firm.

Put the tart shells on a serving platter and spoon the lime mixture into each shell. Mix the mango with the papaya and, using a teaspoon, top the tarts. Decorate with lime zest and serve immediately.

For summer berry tartlets, make the pastry shells and filling as above. Spoon the filling into the cases. Warm 3 tablespoons red currant jelly with the grated zest and juice of 1 lime, cook until syrupy, then stir in 1¼ cups blueberries and 1¼ cups raspberries. Spoon over the top of the tartlets.

deliciously
decadent

strawberry rosé jelly & syllabub

Serves **6**

Preparation time **25 minutes**, plus soaking and chilling

4 tablespoons **water**

1 envelope or 3 teaspoons **powdered gelatin**

3 tablespoons **superfine sugar**

2 cups **rosé wine**

1½ cups small **strawberries**, hulled and halved

Syllabub cream

finely grated zest of 1 **lemon**

2 tablespoons **superfine sugar**

6 tablespoons **rosé wine**

1 cup **heavy cream**

Spoon the measured water into a small heatproof bowl or mug, then sprinkle the gelatin over the top, tilting the bowl so that the dry powder is completely absorbed by the water. Allow to soak for 5 minutes.

Heat the bowl or mug in a small pan of simmering water for 5 minutes or until a clear liquid forms. Take off the heat, then stir in the sugar until dissolved. Cool slightly, then gradually mix into the rosé wine.

Divide the strawberries between 6 tall Champagne-style glasses. Pour the rosé jelly mixture over and chill in the refrigerator until the jelly is set.

Mix the lemon zest, sugar, and wine for the syllabub together and set aside. When ready to serve, whip the cream until it forms soft swirls, then gradually beat in the lemon zest mixture. Spoon over the jellies.

For mimosa jellies, dissolve the gelatin as above, add 2 tablespoons superfine sugar, and when cool mix in ¾ cup blood (or ordinary) orange juice and 2 cups cheap dry sparkling white wine. Divide 1¼ cups fresh or frozen raspberries between the glasses, then top up with the jelly. Chill until set and serve plain.

chilled black currant & mint soufflé

Serves **6**
Preparation time **40 minutes**,
  plus chilling
Cooking time **18–20 minutes**

2 cups **black currants**,
  defrosted if frozen
6 tablespoons **water**
4 teaspoons **powdered**
  gelatin
4 **eggs**, separated
1 cup **superfine sugar**
1 cup **heavy cream**
5 tablespoons finely chopped
  fresh mint
confectioners' sugar, for
  dusting

Wrap a double thickness strip of nonstick parchment paper around a 5½ inch diameter x 2½ inch deep soufflé dish so the paper stands 2½ inches above the dish top. In a saucepan, put the black currants and 2 tablespoons of the water, cover, and cook gently for 5 minutes until softened. Blend until smooth, then press through a sieve.

Put the remaining water in a small heatproof bowl and sprinkle over the gelatin, making sure the water absorbs all the powder. Set aside for 5 minutes, then stand the bowl in a pan half-filled with boiling water and simmer for 3–4 minutes, stirring occasionally, until the gelatin dissolves to a clear liquid.

Put the yolks and sugar in a large heatproof bowl and place over a pan of simmering water so the bowl's base is not touching the water. Beat for 10 minutes or until the eggs are very thick and pale, and leave a trail when lifted above the mixture. Remove from the heat and continue beating until cool. Fold in the dissolved gelatin in a thin, steady stream, then fold in the puree.

Whip the cream softly, then fold into the soufflé mix with the mint. Beat the whites into stiff, moist-looking peaks. Fold a large spoonful into the soufflé mixture to loosen it, then gently fold in the remaining whites. Pour the mixture into the soufflé dish so that it stands above the rim of the dish. Chill for 4 hours or until set.

Remove the string and paper. Arrange 4–5 strips of nonstick parchment paper over the top so some overlap, then dust with sifted confectioners' sugar. Lift off the strips and serve immediately or the sugar will dissolve.

summer berry sponge cake

Serves **6–8**
Preparation time **30 minutes**,
   plus cooling
Cooking time **10–12 minutes**

4 eggs
½ cup **superfine sugar**
1 cup **all-purpose flour**
finely grated zest and
   2 tablespoons juice of
   1 lemon
⅔ cup **heavy cream**
⅔ cup **plain yogurt**
3 tablespoons **lemon curd**
3 cups small **strawberries**,
   halved
1¼ cups **blueberries**
4 tablespoons **red currant
   jelly**
1 tablespoon **water** (or **lemon
   juice**)

Beat the eggs and superfine sugar in a large bowl until very thick and the mixture leaves a trail when lifted. Sift the flour over the surface of the eggs, then fold in very gently. Add the lemon zest and juice and fold in until just mixed. Pour the mixture into a greased, floured 10 inch sponge cake tart pan, tilting the pan to ease into an even layer.

Bake in a preheated oven, 350°F, for 10–12 minutes until the top is golden and the center springs back when lightly pressed. Cool the cake in the pan for 5–10 minutes, then carefully turn it out onto a cooling rack to cool.

Whip the cream until it forms soft swirls, then fold in the plain yogurt and lemon curd. Transfer the cake to a serving plate, spoon the cream into the center, spread into an even layer, then top with the strawberries and blueberries. Warm the red currant jelly in a small saucepan with the measured water (or lemon juice), then brush over the fruit.

For strawberry sponge cake tart with Pimm's, make the sponge cake tart as above, then fill with 1¼ cups whipped cream flavored with the grated zest of ½ orange. Top with 3 cups sliced strawberries and 1¼ cups raspberries that have been soaked in 3 tablespoons undiluted Pimm's and 2 tablespoons superfine sugar for 30 minutes.

hazelnut meringue gateau

Serves **8–10**
Preparation time **30 minutes**,
  plus cooling and chilling
Cooking time **1–1¼ hours**

5 **eggs**, separated
1¼ cups **superfine sugar**
1 tablespoon **cornstarch**
1 cup **blanched hazelnuts**,
  toasted and finely ground
8 oz **bittersweet chocolate**,
  broken into pieces
¾ cup **heavy cream**
cocoa powder, for dusting

Chocolate hazelnuts
2 oz **bittersweet chocolate**,
  broken into pieces
⅓ cup **hazelnuts**

Line 3 baking sheets and draw a 9 inch circle on each piece of parchment paper.

Beat the egg whites until stiff, then gradually beat in the sugar until thick and glossy (see page 10). Fold in the cornstarch and ground hazelnuts until evenly incorporated and transfer the mixture to a large pastry bag fitted with a ½ inch plain tip. Starting in the center of each prepared circle, pipe the mixture in a continuous coil, finishing just within the marked line.

Bake in a preheated oven, 300°F, for 1–1¼ hours until lightly golden and dried out. Remove from the oven and transfer to a cooling rack to cool completely. Peel away the parchment paper.

Melt the chocolate (see page 11) together with the cream over a pan of gently simmering water to make the filling. Cool, then chill for 1 hour until thickened.

Melt the chocolate for the chocolate hazelnuts and use a fork to dip in the hazelnuts until coated. Allow to set on parchment paper.

Beat the chocolate filling until it is light and fluffy and use to sandwich the meringue layers together. Decorate the gateau with the chocolate hazelnuts and serve dusted with sifted cocoa powder.

For chocolate & almond gateau, replace the ground hazelnuts with 1 cup ground almonds and fold into the egg whites and sugar with the cornstarch. Bake the meringue and fill as above. Coat ½ cup blanched almonds in melted chocolate and use as above, finishing with a dusting of cocoa powder.

summer berry mousses

Serves **6**
Preparation time **45 minutes**,
  plus cooling and chilling
Cooking time **12–15 minutes**

3 **eggs**
⅓ cup **superfine sugar**
¾ cup **all-purpose flour**, sifted

Mousse
2 teaspoons **powdered
  gelatin**
2 tablespoons **cold water**
2 **egg whites**
⅓ cup **superfine sugar**
⅔ cup **heavy cream**
1½ cups **frozen summer
  fruits**, just defrosted, pureed

To decorate
a few whole **red currants** and
  raspberries and some
  strawberries, halved
a few small **fresh mint leaves**
confectioners' sugar, for
  dusting

Beat the eggs and sugar until they are very thick and the whisk leaves a trail when lifted. Gently fold in the flour. Line the base and sides of a pan with a 14 x 10 inch base. Pour in the batter.

Bake in a preheated oven, 350°F, for 12–15 minutes until the cake is golden and springs back when pressed. Allow to cool in the pan.

Cut 12 x 3 inch circles from the cake with a cookie cutter. Cut 6 strips of plastic (a new plastic folder is ideal) measuring 11 x 3 inches. Wrap a strip tightly around each of the cake circles and secure with tape. Put on a baking sheet.

Sprinkle gelatin over the measured water in a bowl and allow to soak for 5 minutes. Stand the bowl in a pan of simmering water and leave until the gelatin has dissolved to a clear liquid. Beat the egg whites until stiff peaks form, then gradually beat in the sugar until thick and glossy (see page 10). Whip the cream in a second bowl. Trickle the gelatin into the cream and mix together, then fold in the fruit puree and meringue.

Divide the mixture between the plastic collars, then top with the remaining cake circles. Chill the mousses for 4–5 hours until set. Remove the plastic, sprinkle each mousse with a few whole or halved berries, dust with sifted confectioners' sugar, and serve.

For peach melba mousses, make the mousses with 4 ripe peaches, pureed and sieved. Chill as above, then serve drizzled with 1 cup pureed, sieved raspberries and a few extra whole raspberries.

baked ricotta cheesecake

Serves **6**

Preparation time **20 minutes**, plus cooling and chilling

Cooking time **47–50 minutes**

2 cups **ricotta cheese**

1¾ cups **cream cheese**

2 **eggs**

1 teaspoon **vanilla extract**

½ cup **superfine sugar**

½ small **orange**

1 teaspoon **whole cloves**

2 tablespoons **dark brown sugar**

1 **cinnamon stick**

¾ cup **water**

12 oz **red plums**, halved and pitted

2 tablespoons **red currant jelly**

Grease a 1 lb loaf pan lightly and line the base and sides with nonstick parchment paper. Blend the ricotta and cream cheese with the eggs, vanilla extract, and superfine sugar until smooth. Turn the mixture into the loaf pan and place in a small roasting pan. Pour hot water into the pan to a depth of 1 inch and bake in a preheated oven, 325°F, for about 40 minutes or until lightly set. Lift the loaf pan out of the water and allow to cool in the pan.

Stud the orange with the cloves and place in a heavy pan with the brown sugar, cinnamon, and measured water. Bring the water to a boil, reduce the heat, and add the plums. Cover and cook gently for 5 minutes or until just tender.

Lift out the plums and add the red currant jelly to the pan. Boil the liquid for about 2 minutes until reduced and syrupy. Remove the orange and cinnamon stick and pour the syrup over the plums. Let the syrup cool, then chill until ready to serve.

Remove the cheesecake from the pan, peel off the paper, and cut into slices. Serve topped with the poached plums.

For baked ricotta cheesecake with tropical sauce, make the cheesecake as above, omitting the poached plums. Roughly chop the flesh of 1 large mango, then puree with the juice of 1 large orange and 1 lime. Sieve the puree, then mix with 1 tablespoon confectioners' sugar and the seeds from 2 halved passion fruits. Serve with cheesecake slices.

lemon cornmeal cake

Serves **8–10**

Preparation time **20 minutes**, plus cooling

Cooking time **30 minutes**

1 cup **all-purpose flour**
1½ teaspoons **baking powder**
¾ cup **cornmeal**
3 **eggs**
2 **egg whites**
¾ cup **superfine sugar**
grated zest and juice of
    2 **lemons**
6 tablespoons **vegetable oil**
⅔ cup **buttermilk**

Red wine strawberries
1¼ cups **red wine**
1 **vanilla bean**, split
⅔ cup **superfine sugar**
2 tablespoons **balsamic
    vinegar**
1½ cups **strawberries**, hulled

Sift the flour and baking powder into a bowl and stir in the cornmeal, then set aside. Beat the eggs, egg whites, and sugar together for 3–4 minutes until pale and thickened. Stir in the cornmeal mixture, lemon zest and juice, oil, and buttermilk to form a smooth batter.

Pour the batter into a greased and base-lined 10 inch springform cake pan. Bake in a preheated oven, 350°F, for 30 minutes until risen and firm to the touch. Allow to cool in the pan for 10 minutes, then turn out onto a cooling rack, remove the lining paper, and allow to cool.

Place the wine, vanilla bean, and sugar in a saucepan and heat gently to dissolve the sugar. Increase the heat and simmer for 10–15 minutes until the mixture is reduced and syrupy. Allow to cool, then stir in the balsamic vinegar and strawberries.

Cut the lemon cornmeal cake into slices and serve with the red wine strawberries.

For cornmeal cake with lemon syrup, make up the cake as above. In a saucepan, heat the finely grated zest and juice of 2 lemons, 1 cup superfine sugar, and 2 tablespoons of water, until the sugar has dissolved. Turn the hot cake out onto a serving plate, pour over the syrup, and allow to soak for 15 minutes. Serve warm, in wedges, with cream or whole milk yogurt.

coffee latte custards

Serves **6**
Preparation time **20 minutes**,
  plus chilling
Cooking time **30 minutes**

2 **eggs**
2 **egg yolks**
1⅛ cups **full-fat condensed
  milk**
¾ cup **strong black coffee**
⅔ cup **heavy cream**
cocoa powder, for dusting
chocolate wafer cookies,
  to serve

Beat the eggs, egg yolks, and condensed milk in a bowl until just mixed. Gradually beat in the coffee until blended.

Strain the mixture, then pour into 6 greased small (approximately ½ cup) coffee cups. Transfer the cups to a roasting pan. Pour hot water into the pan to come halfway up the sides of the cups, then cook in a preheated oven, 325°F, for 30 minutes until just set. Lift the cups out of the water, allow to cool, then transfer to the refrigerator and chill for 4–5 hours.

Whip the cream until it forms soft swirls when ready to serve. Spoon the cream over the top of the desserts, dust with a little sifted cocoa powder, and serve with chocolate wafer cookies.

For dark chocolate custards, bring 1¾ cups milk and ⅔ cup heavy cream just to a boil in a saucepan. Add 7 oz bittersweet chocolate, broken into pieces, and allow to melt. Mix 2 eggs and 2 egg yolks with ¼ cup superfine sugar and ¼ teaspoon ground cinnamon, then gradually mix in the chocolate mixture and stir until smooth. Strain into small dishes and bake as above. Top with whipped cream and chocolate curls.

choc & chestnut roulade

Serves **8**

Preparation time **20 minutes**,
  plus cooling

Cooking time **25 minutes**

4 oz **bittersweet chocolate**,
  broken into pieces

5 **eggs**, separated

¾ cup **superfine sugar**, plus
  extra to sprinkle

2 tablespoons **cocoa powder**,
  sifted

8 oz can **unsweetened
  chestnut puree**

4 tablespoons **confectioners'
  sugar**

1 tablespoon **brandy**

1 cup **heavy cream**

confectioners' sugar, for
  dusting

Melt the chocolate (see page 11), then allow to cool for 5 minutes. Put the egg yolks in a bowl, add the sugar, and beat together for 5 minutes until pale and thickened. Stir in the melted chocolate and cocoa. Beat the egg whites in a clean bowl until stiff and fold into the chocolate mixture until evenly combined.

Grease and line a 13 x 9 inch jelly roll pan. Transfer the mixture to the pan, spreading it well into the corners, and smooth the surface with a spatula. Bake in a preheated oven, 350°F, for 20 minutes until risen and set.

Sprinkle a large sheet of parchment paper with superfine sugar. Remove the roulade from the oven and turn it out immediately onto the sugared paper. Carefully remove the lining paper and cover the roulade with a clean dish towel. Set aside to cool.

Put the chestnut puree and confectioners' sugar in a food processor and puree until smooth (or combine well by hand). Transfer the mixture to a bowl and stir in the brandy. Gently beat in the cream until light and fluffy. Spread the filling over the roulade, leaving a ½ inch border, and roll it up from one short end to form a log. Serve dusted with sifted confectioners' sugar.

For Black Forest roulade, make and bake the roulade as above. Whip the heavy cream until it forms soft swirls, then beat in 2 tablespoons confectioners' sugar and 2 tablespoons kirsch, if desired. Spread over the roulade, then sprinkle with a 14 oz can of pitted cherries, well drained. Roll up the roulade and dust with confectioners' sugar.

amaretti & chocolate custard

Serves **4**

Preparation time **20 minutes**,
  plus chilling

Cooking time **55–65 minutes**

¾ cup **granulated sugar**

½ cup **cold water**

2 tablespoons **cocoa powder**

4 tablespoons **boiling water**

2 **eggs**

2 **egg yolks**

¾ cup finely crushed **amaretti
  cookies**

1¾ cups **milk**

⅔ cup **strong black coffee**

To decorate

chocolate curls or a few
  amaretti cookies, crumbled

Dissolve ½ cup sugar in the water, occasionally stirring. When dissolved, increase the heat and boil for 5 minutes without stirring until golden brown, keeping a watchful eye toward the end of the cooking time.

Mix the cocoa in a small bowl with 2 tablespoons of the boiling water. Mix the remaining sugar with the eggs, egg yolks, and crumbs in a second larger bowl.

Take the syrup off the heat as soon as it caramelizes. Add the remaining boiling water and tilt to mix. Pour into a 4 cup ovenproof china dish. Tilt to coat the base and halfway up the sides. Stand in a roasting pan.

Pour the milk into the drained caramel pan and bring just to a boil. Stir the cocoa mix into the egg mixture, then gradually beat in the hot milk, then the coffee. Slowly pour into the caramel-lined dish.

Fill the pan with hot water halfway up the sides of the dish, then cook in a preheated oven, 325°F, for 50–60 minutes until the custard has just set but still wobbles slightly in the center.

Take the dish out of the pan, cool, then chill for 4–5 hours or overnight. To turn out, stand in just-boiled water for 10 seconds, then invert on a plate with a rim. Decorate with chocolate curls or crumbled cookies.

For crème caramels, make the caramel as above. Mix 2 whole eggs and 2 egg yolks with 2 tablespoons sugar and ½ teaspoon vanilla extract. Warm 2½ cups milk, beat into the eggs, then divide among 4 individual 1 cup metal molds. Cook as above in a roasting pan of water for 30 minutes. Cool and chill.

hazelnut & pear roulade

Serves **6–8**

Preparation time **30 minutes**, plus cooling

Cooking time **18–20 minutes**

1 cup **hazelnuts**

5 **eggs**, separated

¾ cup **superfine sugar**, plus extra for sprinkling

1 just-ripe **pear**, peeled and coarsely grated

¾ cup **mascarpone cheese**

2 tablespoons **confectioners' sugar**

8 oz **fresh apricots**, roughly chopped

Grease and line a 12 x 9 inch roasting pan with nonstick parchment paper, snipping diagonally into the corners so it lines the base and sides. Place the nuts on a piece of foil and toast under the broiler for 3–4 minutes until golden. Roughly chop 2 tablespoons and reserve for decoration, then finely chop the remainder.

Beat the yolks and sugar until they are thick and pale and the whisk leaves a trail. Fold in the finely chopped hazelnuts and pear. Beat the whites into stiff, moist-looking peaks. Fold a large spoonful into the nut mix to loosen it, then gently fold in the remaining egg whites.

Spoon the mixture into the prepared pan. Bake the roulade in a preheated oven, 350°F, for 15 minutes until golden brown and the top feels spongy. Cover and allow to cool for at least 1 hour.

Beat the mascarpone and confectioners' sugar together until soft. Cover a damp dish towel with parchment paper, sprinkle with sugar, then turn the roulade onto the paper and remove the pan and lining paper.

Spread the roulade with the mascarpone mixture, then with the apricots. Roll up the roulade, starting from the short end nearest you, using the paper and dish towel to help. Transfer the roulade to a serving plate, sprinkle with the reserved hazelnuts, and cut into thick slices.

For hazelnut, pear, & chocolate roulade, make the roulade as above. Warm ⅔ cup chocolate and hazelnut spread in the microwave for 20 seconds, then gently spread over the roulade. Whip 1 cup heavy cream, spoon over the top, then roll up.

134

gooseberry fool with lemon thins

Serves **6**
Preparation time **30 minutes**,
  plus cooling
Cooking time **20–25 minutes**

3 cups **gooseberries**, topped
  and tailed
⅓ cup **superfine sugar**
2 tablespoons **concentrated
  elderflower cordial**
2 tablespoons **water**
⅔ cup **heavy cream**
4½ oz can or carton **custard**

Lemon thins
¼ cup **unsalted butter**
¼ cup **superfine sugar**
2 tablespoons **corn syrup**
grated zest 1 **lemon**, plus
  1 tablespoon of the juice
1 cup **all-purpose flour**
½ teaspoon **baking soda**
confectioners' sugar, for
  dusting

Cook the gooseberries with the sugar, cordial, and measured water in a covered saucepan for 10 minutes until soft. Puree the gooseberries and their cooking juices in a blender or food processor until smooth, or rub through a sieve. Let cool.

Whip the cream until it forms soft swirls, then fold in the custard and gooseberry puree. Spoon into small glasses and chill.

Heat the butter, sugar, syrup, and lemon zest and juice for the cookies in a small saucepan until the butter has melted and sugar dissolved. Stir in the flour and baking soda and mix until smooth.

Drop teaspoons of the mixture onto 2 greased baking sheets, well spaced apart, then bake in a preheated oven, 350°F, for 10–12 minutes until browning around the edges. Cool for 10 minutes, then loosen and transfer to a cooling rack. Dust the lemon thins with sifted confectioners' sugar and serve with the fool.

For nectarine & orange fool, chop the flesh of 4 ripe nectarines, then cook them in a covered saucepan with the sugar and 4 tablespoons of fresh orange juice (no water or cordial) for 10 minutes until tender. Puree and finish as above. Add the grated zest of ½ orange and 1 tablespoon juice to the cookies instead of the lemon.

strawberry & lavender soufflés

Serves **6**
Preparation time **40 minutes**,
  plus chilling
Cooking time **13–14 minutes**

3 cups **fresh strawberries**,
  hulled
4 tablespoons **water**
4 teaspoons **powdered
  gelatin**
4 **eggs**, separated
⅔ cup **superfine sugar**
4–5 **lavender sprigs**, petals
  crumbled and stems
  discarded
1 cup **heavy cream**
few drops **pink** or **red food
  coloring** (optional)
small bunch **lavender**, to
  decorate

Attach soufflé collars to 6 individual soufflé dishes,
3 inches in diameter, 1½ inches deep, so that the paper
rises 1½ inches above the top. Slice 6 strawberries and
divide them among the dishes. Blend the remaining
strawberries to a coarse puree.

Pour the measured water into a small heatproof bowl
and sprinkle with the gelatin. Set aside for 5 minutes,
then stand the bowl in a pan half-filled with boiling
water and simmer for 3–4 minutes, stirring occasionally,
until the gelatin dissolves to a clear liquid.

Put the egg yolks, sugar, and lavender petals in a large
heatproof bowl and stand over a pan of simmering
water so the base does not touch the water. Beat with
a hand-held electric mixer (or rotary hand or balloon
whisk) for 10 minutes or until the eggs are very thick
and pale and the whisk leaves a trail. Remove the bowl
from the heat and continue beating until cool.

Gradually fold in the dissolved gelatin in a thin, steady
stream, then fold in the strawberry puree.

Softly whip the cream, then fold into the soufflé
mixture with the food coloring, if using. Chill if the
mixture is very soft.

Beat the egg whites into stiff, moist-looking peaks.
Fold a large spoonful into the soufflé mixture to loosen
it, then gently fold in the remaining egg whites. Pour
the mixture into the prepared soufflé dishes so that it
stands above the rim. Chill for 4 hours or until set.

Peel back the paper collars and tuck a few trimmed
lavender stems under the string to serve.

pavlovas with orange cream

Serves **6**
Preparation time **25 minutes**,
 plus cooling
Cooking time **1¼–1½ hours**

4 oz **bittersweet chocolate**,
 broken into pieces, plus a
 little extra, grated, to
 decorate
3 **egg whites**
6 oz **superfine sugar**
1 teaspoon **cornstarch**
1 teaspoon **white wine
 vinegar**
½ teaspoon **vanilla extract**
1 cup **heavy cream**
2 **oranges**

Melt the chocolate (see page 11), then allow to cool for 10 minutes. Beat the egg whites in a large bowl until stiff, moist-looking peaks form. Gradually beat in the sugar and continue to beat until the meringue is thick and glossy (see page 10).

Mix the cornstarch with the vinegar and vanilla extract, then fold into the meringue. Add the melted chocolate and fold together briefly for a marbled effect. Spoon the meringue into 6 mounds on a large baking sheet lined with nonstick parchment paper, then swirl into circles with the back of the spoon, making a slight indentation in the center.

Bake in a preheated oven, 225°F, for 1¼–1½ hours or until the pavlovas may be easily lifted off the paper. Allow to cool.

Whip the cream, when ready to serve, until it forms soft swirls. Grate the zest of 1 orange and fold into the cream. Slice off the top and bottom of each orange, then cut away the rest of the peel. Remove the segments, add any juice to the cream, then spoon this over the pavlovas. Arrange the segments and grate a little dark chocolate on top.

For strawberry & litchi pavlovas, make the meringue as above, omitting the chocolate, and bake for just 50–60 minutes. Fill with 1 cup whipped heavy cream flavored with the grated zest of 1 lime and 2 tablespoons confectioners' sugar. Top with a 14 oz can pitted litchis, drained and quartered, and 1½ cups sliced strawberries.

vanilla crème brûlée

Serves **6**

Preparation time **20 minutes**,
    plus standing and chilling

Cooking time **25–30 minutes**

1 **vanilla bean**

2½ cups **heavy cream**

8 **egg yolks**

5 tablespoons **superfine sugar**

3 tablespoons **confectioners' sugar**

Slit the vanilla bean lengthwise and place it in a saucepan. Pour the cream into the pan, then bring almost to a boil. Take off the heat and allow to stand for 15 minutes. Lift the bean out of the cream and, holding it against the side of the saucepan, scrape the black seeds into the cream. Discard the rest of the bean.

Use a fork to mix together the egg yolks and superfine sugar in a bowl. Reheat the cream, then gradually mix it into the eggs and sugar. Strain the mixture back into the saucepan.

Place 6 ovenproof ramekins in a roasting pan, then divide the custard between them. Pour warm water around the dishes to come halfway up the sides, then bake in a preheated oven, 350°F, for 20–25 minutes until the custard is just set with a slight softness at the center.

Allow the dishes to cool in the water, then lift out and chill in the refrigerator for 3–4 hours. About 25 minutes before serving, sprinkle with the confectioners' sugar and caramelize using a kitchen torch (or under a hot broiler), then leave at room temperature.

For Amaretto brûlée, omit the vanilla bean. Mix the egg yolks and sugar as above, bring the cream almost to a boil, then immediately mix into the egg yolks adding ½ cup Amaretto di Saronno liqueur. Strain and continue as above. When chilled, sprinkle with 6 teaspoons slivered almonds, then the sugar, and caramelize as above.

blueberry & cherry cheesecake

Serves **6**

Preparation time **30 minutes**, plus chilling

Cooking time **5 minutes**

⅓ cup **unsalted butter**

2 tablespoons **corn syrup**

2 cups crushed **graham crackers**

1¼ cups **full-fat cream cheese**

¾ cup **fat-free fromage frais** or **plain yogurt**

¼ cup **superfine sugar**

grated zest and juice of 1 **lemon**

½ teaspoon **vanilla extract**

⅔ cup **heavy cream**

Topping

1¼ cups **frozen blueberries**

⅔ cup **frozen pitted cherries**

4 tablespoons **water**

2 tablespoons **superfine sugar**

2 teaspoons **cornstarch**

Melt the butter in a saucepan with the corn syrup, then stir in the cracker crumbs and mix well. Tip the mixture into a greased 8 inch springform pan and press over the base and two-thirds of the way up the sides with the back of a spoon. Chill.

Scoop the cream cheese into a mixing bowl and break down with a spoon. Stir in the fromage frais or yogurt, sugar, lemon zest and vanilla extract, then gradually mix in the lemon juice until smooth.

Beat the cream in a second bowl until it forms soft swirls, then fold into the cheese mixture. Pour into the crumb-lined pan and spread the surface level. Chill for 4–5 hours or overnight until firm.

Warm the frozen fruits in a pan with the measured water and sugar for 3–4 minutes until defrosted. Blend the cornstarch with a little extra water, add to the pan, bring to a boil, stirring, and cook for 1 minute until the sauce has thickened. Allow to cool.

Loosen the edge of the crumb shell when ready to serve, unclip the pan sides, lift off the base, and transfer the cheesecake to a serving plate. Cut into wedges and serve with the fruit compote drizzled over the top.

For lime, kiwifruit, & grape cheesecake, add the grated zest and juice of 2 limes to the cheesecake mixture instead of the lemon. Spoon into the pan as above, then arrange 2 sliced kiwifruits and 1 cup halved green and red seedless grapes in rings over the top while the filling is still soft. Chill until set, then remove from the pan and cut into wedges to serve.

raspberry & champagne brûlée

Serves **6**

Preparation time **20 minutes**, plus cooling

Cooking time **25 minutes**

2 cups **fresh raspberries**, plus a few extra, dusted with **confectioners' sugar**, to decorate (optional)

6 **egg yolks**

⅔ cup **superfine sugar**

½ cup **dry Champagne**

½ cup **heavy cream**

3 tablespoons **confectioners' sugar**

Divide the raspberries among 6 ramekin dishes. Put the egg yolks and sugar in a large bowl and set it over a saucepan of simmering water, making sure the water does not touch the bottom of the bowl. Beat the egg yolks and sugar until light and foamy, then gradually beat in the Champagne, then the cream. Continue beating for about 20 minutes until the custard is very thick and bubbly.

Pour the custard over the raspberries and allow to cool at room temperature for about 1 hour. Sprinkle the tops with the sifted confectioners' sugar and caramelize with a kitchen torch (or under a hot broiler). Serve within 20–30 minutes, decorated with a few extra raspberries lightly dusted with confectioners' sugar.

For cidered peach brûlée, divide the diced flesh of 2 ripe peaches among 6 ramekins. Beat the egg yolks and sugar as above, then gradually beat in ½ cup hard cider instead of the Champagne. Continue as above.

146

gingered pineapple trifle

Serves **4–5**
Preparation time **20 minutes**

7 oz **Jamaican gingercake**, diced
½ **fresh pineapple**, sliced, cored, peeled, and diced
grated zest and segmented flesh of **1 orange**
2 **kiwifruits**, peeled, halved, and sliced
3 tablespoons **rum**
14 oz can or carton **custard**
1¼ cups **heavy cream**
grated zest of **1 lime**

Arrange the gingercake in an even layer in the base of a 5 cup glass serving dish. Spoon the pineapple, orange segments, and kiwifruits on top and drizzle with the rum. Pour the custard over the fruit and spread into an even layer.

Whip the cream in a bowl until it forms soft swirls, then fold in half the orange zest and half the lime zest. Spoon the cream over the custard, then sprinkle with the remaining fruit zests. Chill until ready to serve.

For raspberry & peach trifle, dice 4 slices of pound cake and sprinkle in the base of a glass dish instead of the gingercake. Add 1¼ cups fresh raspberries and the diced flesh of 2 ripe peaches. Drizzle with 3 tablespoons dry sherry, then cover with custard as above. Whip the cream and flavor with the grated zest of 1 lemon, spoon it over the custard, and sprinkle with 2 tablespoons toasted slivered almonds.

florentine vanilla cheesecake

Serves **8–10**

Preparation time **25 minutes**, plus chilling

Cooking time **45 minutes**

4 oz **bittersweet chocolate**

½ cup **slivered almonds**, lightly toasted

2½ tablespoons **candied citron**, finely chopped

6 **candied cherries**, finely chopped

2 cups crushed **graham crackers**

5 tablespoons **unsalted butter**, melted

2 cups **cream cheese**

1 teaspoon **vanilla extract**

⅔ cup **heavy cream**

⅔ cup **Greek** or **whole milk yogurt**

½ cup **superfine sugar**

3 **eggs**

Grease an 8 inch removable-bottomed cake pan and line the sides with a strip of nonstick parchment paper. Chop half the chocolate into small pieces. Lightly crush the almonds and mix them in a bowl with the chocolate, candied fruit, cracker crumbs, and butter. Stir the mixture until well combined, then turn into the pan, packing it into the bottom and slightly up the sides to form a shell.

Beat the cream cheese and vanilla extract in a bowl until smooth. Beat in the cream, yogurt, sugar, and eggs to make a smooth batter.

Pour the egg mixture over the crumb base and bake in a preheated oven, 325°F, for 45 minutes or until the surface feels just firm around the edges but is still wobbly in the center. Turn off the heat and let the cheesecake cool in the oven. Transfer to the refrigerator and chill well.

Transfer to a serving plate and peel away the lining paper. Melt the remaining chocolate (see page 11) and drizzle it around the top edges of the cheesecake. Chill until ready to serve.

For American cherry cheesecake, make a plain crumb shell by heating ⅓ cup butter together with 2 tablespoons corn syrup in a pan until the butter has melted. Stir in 2 cups crushed graham crackers and use to line the pan as above. Make the filling and bake as above. Serve topped with a 14 oz can of cherry pie filling.

rosemary panna cottas

Serves **6**
Preparation time **15 minutes**,
   plus soaking and chilling
Cooking time **15 minutes**

3 tablespoons **cold water**
1 envelope or 3 teaspoons
   powdered gelatin
1¾ cups **heavy cream**
⅔ cup **milk**
4 tablespoons **honey**
2 teaspoons very finely
   chopped **rosemary leaves**

Apricot compote

1¼ cups ready-to-eat **dried
   apricots**, sliced
1¼ cups **water**
1 tablespoon **honey**
2 teaspoons very finely
   chopped **rosemary leaves**

To decorate

small **rosemary sprigs**
superfine sugar, for dusting

Spoon the measured water into a small heatproof bowl or mug. Sprinkle the gelatin over and tilt the bowl or mug so that all the dry powder is absorbed by the water. Allow to soak for 5 minutes.

Pour the cream and milk into a saucepan, add the honey, and bring to a boil. Add the soaked gelatin, take the pan off the heat, and stir until completely dissolved. Add the rosemary and leave for 20 minutes for the flavors to infuse, stirring from time to time. Pour the cream mixture into 6 individual ⅔ cup metal molds, straining if preferred. Allow to cool completely, then chill for 4–5 hours until set.

Put all the compote ingredients into a saucepan, cover, and simmer for 10 minutes, then allow to cool.

Dip the molds into hot water for 10 seconds, loosen the edges, then turn out the panna cottas onto small serving plates and spoon the compote around them. Lightly dust the rosemary sprigs with superfine sugar and use to decorate the panna cottas.

For vanilla panna cottas, make the panna cotta as above but without the rosemary, adding the seeds from 1 slit vanilla bean and the pod as the cream mixture cools. Discard the pod just before pouring the mixture into the molds, then continue as above. Turn out and serve with fresh raspberries.

pink grapefruit cream

Serves **4**
Preparation time **15 minutes**

2 pink **grapefruits**
5 tablespoons **dark brown sugar**, plus extra for sprinkling
1 cup **heavy cream**
⅔ cup **Greek** or **whole milk yogurt**
3 tablespoons **concentrated elderflower cordial**
½ teaspoon **ground ginger**
½ teaspoon **ground cinnamon**
brandy snaps, to serve (optional)

Grate the zest of 1 grapefruit finely, making sure you don't take any of the bitter white pith. Cut the skin and the white membrane off both grapefruits, and cut between the membranes to remove the segments. Place in a large dish, sprinkle with 2 tablespoons of the sugar, and set aside.

Beat the cream in a large bowl until thick but not stiff. Fold in the yogurt, elderflower cordial, spices, grapefruit zest, and remaining sugar until smooth.

Spoon the mixture into attractive glasses, arranging the grapefruit segments between layers of grapefruit cream. Sprinkle the top with a little extra sugar, add the brandy snaps, if desired, and serve immediately.

For spiced orange cream, finely grate the zest of 2 large oranges, then cut away the pith and membrane to release the orange segments. Sprinkle with 2 tablespoons of the sugar and set aside. Whip the cream, then flavor as above, adding the orange zest in place of the grapefruit zest.

154

tuile baskets & strawberry cream

Serves **6**
Preparation time **40 minutes**
Cooking time **15–18 minutes**

2 **egg whites**
½ cup **superfine sugar**
¼ cup **unsalted butter**, melted
few drops **vanilla extract**
½ cup **all-purpose flour**

Strawberry cream

1 cup **heavy cream**
4 tablespoons **confectioners'
sugar**, plus extra for dusting
2 tablespoons chopped **fresh
mint**, plus extra leaves to
decorate
1½ cups **strawberries**, halved
or sliced, depending on size

Put the egg whites in a bowl and break up with a fork.
Stir in the superfine sugar, then the butter and vanilla
extract. Sift in the flour and mix until smooth.

Drop 1 heaping tablespoon of the mixture onto a
baking sheet lined with nonstick parchment paper. Drop
a second spoonful well apart from the first, then spread
both into a thin circle about 5 inches in diameter. Bake
in a preheated oven, 375°F, for 5–6 minutes until just
beginning to brown around the edges.

Add 2 more spoonfuls to a second paper-lined baking
sheet and spread thinly. Remove the baked tuiles from
the oven and put in the second tray. Allow the cooked
tuiles to firm up for 5–10 seconds, then carefully
lift them off the paper one at a time and drape each
one over an orange. Pinch the edges into pleats and
allow to harden for 2–3 minutes, then carefully ease
off the oranges. Repeat until 6 tuiles have been made.

Whip the cream lightly, then fold in half the sugar, the
mint, and the strawberries, reserving 6 strawberry
halves for decoration. Spoon into the tuiles, then top
with the mint leaves and the strawberry halves. Dust
with sifted confectioners' sugar.

For fruit salad baskets, make the tuiles as above and
fill with 1⅓ cups sliced strawberries, 1 cup halved
seedless ruby grapes, and 2 kiwifruits plus 2 small
ripe peaches, all peeled, halved, and sliced. Top with
Greek or whole milk yogurt and a drizzle of honey.

156

peach & chocolate vacherin

Serves **6–8**

Preparation time **30 minutes**, plus cooling

Cooking time **1½–1¾ hours**

4 **egg whites**

½ cup **superfine sugar**

½ cup **light brown sugar**

5 oz **bittersweet chocolate**, broken into pieces

Filling

⅔ cup **heavy cream**

⅔ cup **Greek** or **whole milk yogurt**

2 tablespoons **superfine sugar**

3 ripe **peaches**, pitted and sliced

Line 2 baking sheets with nonstick parchment paper and draw a 7 inch circle on each.

Beat the egg whites in a large bowl until stiff, moist-looking peaks form. Mix the sugars together, then beat in the sugar, a teaspoonful at a time, and continue beating for 1–2 minutes until very thick and glossy (see page 10).

Divide the mixture between the lined baking sheets and spread into circles of even thickness between the marked lines. Bake in a preheated oven, 225°F, for 1½–1¾ hours or until the meringues may be easily lifted off the paper. Allow them to cool in the switched-off oven.

Melt the chocolate (see page 11), then spread over the underside of each meringue, leaving about one-third of the chocolate in the bowl for decoration. Allow the meringues to harden, chocolate side up.

Whip the cream, when ready to serve, until it forms soft swirls, then fold in the yogurt and sugar. Put one of the meringue circles on a serving plate, chocolate side up, spread with the cream, then arrange peach slices on top. Cover with the second meringue, chocolate side down. Decorate the top with the remainder of the melted chocolate, drizzled randomly.

For chocolate & chestnut vacherin, make the meringues as above. Spread with chocolate and allow to harden. Whip ⅔ cup heavy cream, fold in a 7½ oz can of sweetened chestnut puree and ⅔ cup fromage frais or plain yogurt, then fill the meringues.

apricot meringue swirl

Serves **8**

Preparation time **35 minutes**, plus cooling

Cooking time **25 minutes**

4 **egg whites**

1 cup **superfine sugar**, plus extra for sprinkling

1 teaspoon **cornstarch**

1 teaspoon **white wine vinegar**

1¼ cups ready-to-eat **dried apricots**

1¼ cups **water**

⅔ cup **heavy cream**

⅔ cup **plain yogurt**

Beat the egg whites until stiff peaks form. Gradually beat in the sugar, then beat for a few minutes more until the mixture is thick and glossy (see page 10).

Mix the cornstarch and vinegar together until smooth. Fold into the meringue mixture.

Spoon into a 13 x 9 inch jelly roll pan lined with nonstick parchment paper snipped diagonally into the corners and standing a little above the top of the sides. Spread level. Bake in a preheated oven, 375°F, for 10 minutes until lightly browned and well risen. Reduce the heat to 325°F and bake for 5 minutes more until just firm to the touch and the top is slightly cracked.

Cover a clean dish towel with nonstick parchment paper and sprinkle with a little sugar. Turn the hot meringue out on to the paper, remove the pan, and let cool for 1–2 hours. Meanwhile, simmer the apricots in the water for 10 minutes until tender. Cool, then puree until smooth.

Peel the lining paper off the meringue when ready to serve, then spread with the apricot puree. Whip the cream until it forms soft swirls, then fold in the fromage frais and spoon over the apricot puree.

Roll up the meringue to make a log shape, starting from a short side and using the paper to help. Transfer to a serving plate and cut into thick slices to serve.

For kiwifruit & passion fruit swirl, make the meringue as above. Fill with 1¼ cups whipped heavy cream, then sprinkle with 3 chopped kiwifruits and the seeds from 3 passion fruits.

chilled out

lime & passion fruit crunch tart

Serves **6–8**

Preparation time **30 minutes**,
  plus chilling and freezing

½ cup **unsalted butter**
2 tablespoons **corn syrup**
3 cups crushed **graham crackers**
1¼ cups **heavy cream**
grated zest and juice of
  3 **limes**
1⅓ cups **full-fat condensed milk**

To decorate
3 **passion fruits**, halved
1¼ cups **blueberries**

Heat the butter and corn syrup in a saucepan, stir in the cracker crumbs, and mix well. Tip into a greased 9 inch springform pan and press over the base of the pan with the end of a rolling pin. Chill the crumb base while making the filling.

Whip the cream in a large bowl until it forms soft swirls. Add the lime zest and condensed milk and gently fold together, then gradually mix in the lime juice. Pour over the crumb base and freeze for 4 hours or overnight.

Loosen the edge of the dessert from the pan with a round-bladed knife, remove the sides, then slide off the base onto a serving plate. Spoon the seeds from the passion fruits over the top, then sprinkle with the blueberries. Allow to soften for 30 minutes before cutting into slices to serve.

For chocolate orange crunch tart, make the crumb base using chocolate-coated cookies. Omit the lime zest and juice from the cream mixture, adding the grated zest and juice from 1 large orange instead. Freeze until solid, then decorate with 2 oz plain dark chocolate, melted (see page 11) and drizzled randomly over the top. Return the dessert to the freezer until required.

pistachio & yogurt semifreddo

Serves **6**

Preparation time **40 minutes**, plus cooling and freezing

Cooking time **10–15 minutes**

4 **eggs**, separated

¾ cup **superfine sugar**

grated zest of 1 **lemon**

1½ teaspoons **rose water** (optional)

¾ cup **Greek** or **whole milk yogurt**

½ **fresh pineapple**, sliced, halved, and cored

Pistachio brittle

⅔ cup **granulated sugar**

6 tablespoons **water**

1 cup **pistachio nuts**, roughly chopped

Make the brittle. Heat the sugar and measured water in a skillet until it dissolves, stirring gently from time to time. Add the nuts, then increase the heat and boil the syrup for 5 minutes, without stirring, until pale golden. Quickly tip the mixture onto a greased baking sheet and allow to cool. Break the brittle in half, then crush half in a plastic bag with a rolling pin.

Beat the egg whites until very stiff, then gradually beat in half the sugar until thick and glossy. Beat the egg yolks in a second bowl with the remaining sugar until very thick and pale and the mixture leaves a trail. Fold in the lemon zest and rose water, if using, then the yogurt and crushed brittle, then the egg whites. Pour into a plastic box and freeze for 4–5 hours until semifrozen and firm enough to scoop.

Cook the pineapple slices on a hot barbecue or preheated griddle pan for 6–8 minutes, turning once or twice until browned. Divide between the serving plates, top with spoonfuls of semifreddo, and decorate with broken pieces of the remaining brittle.

For rocky road ice cream, make the brittle with almonds, hazelnuts, and pecan nuts instead of pistachios. Beat the egg whites, then the eggs and sugar, as for the semifreddo, then fold ½ cup ready-made custard and ⅔ cup whipped heavy cream into the yolks with the crushed brittle. Fold in the egg whites as above, then freeze. Serve scooped into glasses with wafer cookies.

cherry almond ice cream

Serves **6**

Preparation time **20 minutes**,
plus cooling and freezing

Cooking time **20 minutes**

⅔ cup **milk**

½ cup **ground almonds**

1 **egg**

1 **egg yolk**

⅛ cup **superfine sugar**

2–3 drops **almond extract**

3 cups **red cherries**, pitted, or
cherry compote

¼ cup **slivered almonds**

⅔ cup **heavy cream**

Pour the milk into a small saucepan and stir in the
ground almonds. Bring to a boil, then set aside.

Put the egg and the yolk into a heatproof bowl with
the sugar and beat until pale and thick. Pour on the
milk and almond mixture. Place the bowl over a pan of
gently simmering water and stir until thick. Stir in the
almond extract and allow to cool.

Puree the cherries in a food processor or blender (or
use cherry compote), then stir into the custard.

Toss the slivered almonds in a heavy pan over a low
heat to toast them. Allow to cool.

Whip the cream until it forms soft peaks. Fold the
whipped cream into the cherry mixture.

Transfer the mixture to a freezer container, cover, and
freeze until firm, beating twice at hourly intervals. Stir
the slivered almonds into the mixture at the last
beating. (If using an ice-cream machine, pour the
cherry mixture into the machine, add the cream, churn,
and freeze. Once frozen, fold through the slivered
almonds.) Serve the ice cream in individual glasses.

For strawberry & coconut ice cream, soak ¾ cup
shredded coconut in ⅔ cup hot milk. Mix the egg and
egg yolk with sugar and make into custard as above,
omitting the almond extract. When cold, fold in 3 cups
strawberries, pureed, and ⅔ cup whipped heavy cream.
Freeze as above. Serve with extra strawberries.

gingered apricot crush

Serves **6**

Preparation time **25 minutes**, plus cooling and freezing

Cooking time **10 minutes**

1½ cups ready-to-eat **dried apricots**

1¼ cups **water**

1 cup **heavy cream**

¾ cup **fat-free fromage frais** or **plain yogurt**

3 tablespoons **superfine sugar**

3 oz or about 4 pieces **stem ginger** from a jar, drained and roughly chopped, plus 2 tablespoons syrup from jar

1½ oz **ready-made mini meringues**

Put the apricots and measured water in a saucepan, cover, and simmer for 10 minutes. Puree the apricots and cooking liquid in a food processor or blender until smooth, or rub through a sieve. Cool.

Whip the cream in a bowl until it forms soft swirls. Gently fold in the fromage frais or yogurt, superfine sugar, chopped ginger, and ginger syrup. Crumble the meringues into pieces, then fold into the cream.

Line a 2 lb loaf pan with two pieces of plastic wrap at right angles to each other so that the edges overhang the pan. Spoon in alternate spoonfuls of cream and apricot puree. Run the handle of a teaspoon through the mixture to marble together. Then fold the plastic wrap over the top. Freeze for 6 hours or overnight until firm, or longer if preferred.

Unfold the top of the plastic wrap and leave the dessert at room temperature for 15 minutes to soften slightly. Cover with a cutting board, invert the pan onto the board and remove the pan. Peel off the plastic wrap. Cut into thick slices and serve.

For lemon & pineapple crush, flavor the cream mix with the grated zest of 2 lemons and a 7½ oz can of pineapple, drained and finely chopped, instead of the ginger and ginger syrup. Add the meringues as above. Layer in the lined loaf pan with 4 tablespoons lemon curd and marble together. Freeze, then serve sliced with a drizzle of pureed strawberries.

chocolate ice cream

Serves **4**

Preparation time **20 minutes**,
plus cooling and freezing

Cooking time **10 minutes**

1¼ cups **heavy cream**

2 tablespoons **milk**

½ cup **confectioners' sugar**,
sifted

½ teaspoon **vanilla extract**

4 oz good-quality **bittersweet
chocolate**, broken into
pieces

2 tablespoons **light cream**

Chocolate sauce (optional)

⅔ cup **water**

3 tablespoons **superfine
sugar**

5 oz **bittersweet chocolate**,
broken into pieces

Put the heavy cream and milk in a bowl and beat until just stiff. Stir in the confectioners' sugar and vanilla extract. Pour the mixture into a shallow freezer container and freeze for 30 minutes or until the ice cream begins to set around the edges. (This ice cream cannot be made in an ice-cream machine.)

Melt the chocolate (see page 11), together with the light cream, over a pan of gently simmering water. Stir until smooth, then set aside to cool.

Remove the ice cream from the freezer and spoon into a bowl. Add the melted chocolate and quickly stir it through the ice cream with a fork. Return the ice cream to the freezer container, cover, and freeze until set. Transfer the ice cream to the refrigerator 30 minutes before serving, to soften slightly.

Heat all the ingredients for the chocolate sauce, if making, gently in a saucepan, stirring until melted. Serve immediately with scoops of the ice cream.

For chocolate double mint ice cream, make the ice cream as above, adding 2 tablespoons chopped fresh mint and 1 tablespoon crushed peppermint candies to the whipped cream and milk. Freeze as above, then stir in the melted chocolate mix.

litchi & coconut sherbet

Serves **4–6**
Preparation time **30 minutes**,
  plus freezing
Cooking time **2–4 minutes**

14 oz can **pitted litchis in
  light syrup**
¼ cup **superfine sugar**
1¾ cups **full-fat coconut milk**
grated zest and juice of **1 lime**,
  plus extra pared **lime zest**,
  to decorate (optional)
chocolate cups (see below),
  to serve (optional)
3 **kiwifruits**, peeled and cut
  into wedges, to decorate

Drain the syrup from the can of litchis into a saucepan, add the sugar, and heat gently until the sugar has dissolved. Boil for 2 minutes, then take off the heat and allow to cool.

Puree the litchis in a food processor or blender until smooth, or rub through a sieve. Mix with the coconut milk, lime zest, and juice. Stir in the sugar syrup when it is cool.

Pour into a shallow plastic container and freeze for 4 hours or until mushy. Beat with a fork or blend in a food processor or blender until smooth. Pour back into the plastic container and freeze for 4 hours or overnight until solid. (Alternatively, freeze in an electric ice-cream machine for 20 minutes, then transfer to a plastic box and freeze until required.)

Allow to soften for 15 minutes at room temperature before serving, then scoop into dishes or chocolate cups (see below) and decorate with kiwifruit wedges and pared lime zest curls, if desired.

For chocolate cups, to serve the sherbet in, melt 5 oz bittersweet chocolate over a pan of simmering water (see page 11), then divide between 4 squares of nonstick parchment paper and spread into rough-shaped circles about 6 inches in diameter. Drape the paper over upturned glass tumblers, with the chocolate uppermost, so that the paper falls in soft folds. Chill until set, then lift the paper and chocolate off the tumblers, turn over, and carefully ease the paper away.

fresh melon sorbet

Serves **4–6**

Preparation time **15 minutes**,
  plus freezing

1 **cantaloupe melon**,
  weighing 2 lb
½ cup **confectioners' sugar**
juice of **1** **lime** or small **lemon**
1 **egg white**

Cut the melon in half and scoop out and discard the seeds. Scoop out the melon flesh with a spoon and discard the shells.

Place the flesh in a food processor or blender with the confectioners' sugar and lime or lemon juice and process to a puree. (Alternatively, rub through a sieve.) Pour into a freezer container, cover, and freeze for 2–3 hours. If using an ice-cream machine, puree then pour into the machine, churn, and freeze until half-frozen.

Beat the melon mixture to break up the ice crystals. Then beat the egg white until stiff and beat it into the half-frozen melon mixture. Return to the freezer until firm. Alternatively, add the beaten egg white to the ice-cream machine and churn until very thick.

Transfer the sorbet to the refrigerator 20 minutes before serving to soften slightly or scoop it straight from the ice-cream machine. Scoop the sorbet into glass dishes to serve. To make differently colored sorbet, make up three batches of sorbet using a cantaloupe melon in one and honeydew and watermelon in the others.

For gingered melon sorbet, peel and finely grate a 1 inch piece of ginger root, then stir into the melon puree. Scoop into small glasses and drizzle each glass with 1 tablespoon ginger wine.

watermelon & tequila granita

Serves **6**
Preparation time **20 minutes**,
  plus infusing and freezing
Cooking time **2 minutes**

1 **vanilla bean**
⅔ cup **superfine sugar**
⅔ cup **water**
4 lb **watermelon**
2 tablespoons **lemon juice**
4 tablespoons **tequila**

Use a small, sharp knife to score the vanilla bean lengthwise through to the center. Put it in a pan with the sugar and the measured water. Heat gently until the sugar has dissolved and let the syrup infuse for 20 minutes.

Slice the watermelon into wedges and cut away the skin. Blend the flesh in a food processor or blender until smooth, or rub through a sieve.

Remove the vanilla bean from the syrup, scrape out the seeds with the tip of a knife, and return them to the syrup. Beat to disperse them. Discard the pod.

Strain the watermelon puree into a freezer container and stir in the vanilla syrup, lemon juice, and tequila. Freeze for 3–4 hours until it is turning mushy. Mash with a fork and refreeze for 2–3 hours until it reaches the mushy stage again. Repeat the process once or twice more until the granita is evenly mushy. Freeze until required.

Fork through the granita to break up the ice and pile it into tall glasses. Serve with long spoons.

For blackberry and apple granita, heat 1¼ cups water with 2 tablespoons superfine sugar until the sugar has dissolved. Add 4 large Gala apples that have been peeled, cored, and diced and 1 cup blackberries, then cover and simmer for 10 minutes. Cool, then puree and mix with 1¼ cups extra water. Freeze as above until flakes of ice begin to form.

mint granita

Serves **6**
Preparation time **20 minutes**,
  plus cooling and freezing
Cooking time **4 minutes**

1 cup **superfine sugar**
1¼ cups **water**, plus extra to
  top up
pared rind and juice of
  3 lemons
5 tablespoons **fresh mint**,
  plus a few sprigs to
  decorate
confectioners' sugar, for
  dusting

Put the sugar and measured water into a saucepan,
add the lemon rind, and gently heat until the sugar has
dissolved. Increase the heat and boil for 2 minutes.

Tear the tips off the mint stems and finely chop to give
about 3 tablespoons, then reserve. Add the larger mint
leaves and stems to the hot syrup and leave for 1 hour
to cool and for the flavors to develop.

Strain the syrup into a pitcher, add the chopped mint,
and top up to 2½ cups with extra cold water. Pour
into a small roasting pan and freeze the mixture for
2–3 hours or until mushy.

Break up the ice crystals with a fork, then return to
the freezer for 2–3 more hours, breaking up with a
fork once or twice until the mixture is the consistency
of crushed ice. Serve now, spooned into small glass
tumblers, decorated with tiny sprigs of mint dusted
with confectioners' sugar, or leave in the freezer until
required. If leaving in the freezer, allow to soften for
15 minutes before serving. If frozen overnight or longer,
break up with a fork before serving.

For iced ruby grapefruit granita, make a plain sugar
syrup as above, omitting the lemon rind. When cool,
halve 4 ruby grapefruits, squeeze the juice, and
reserve 4 halved shells. Strain the juice into the syrup
instead of the lemon juice, then freeze as above.
Serve the dessert spooned into the reserved
grapefruit shells.

lemon & honey ice

Serves **4–6**

Preparation time **20–25 minutes**, plus cooling and freezing

Cooking time **2 minutes**

4 large or 6 medium **lemons**

about 4 tablespoons **water**

2 tablespoons **honey**

5 tablespoons **superfine sugar**

1 **fresh bay leaf** or **lemon balm** sprig

1¾ cups **plain yogurt** or **fromage frais**

strips of **lemon zest**, to decorate

Slice off the top of each lemon. Carefully scoop out all the pulp and juice with a teaspoon. Discard any white pith, skin, and seeds, then puree the pulp and juice in a food processor or blender, or rub through a sieve. You will need ⅔ cup—if there is less than this, top it up with water.

Put the measured water, honey, sugar, and bay leaf or lemon balm into a saucepan. Stir over a low heat until the sugar has dissolved, then allow to cool. Blend the mixture with the lemon puree and the yogurt or fromage frais. Don't remove the herb at this stage.

Pour into a freezer tray or shallow dish and freeze until lightly frozen, then gently fork the mixture and remove the herb. Return the ice to the freezer until firm.

Transfer to the refrigerator about 20 minutes before serving. Serve decorated with strips of lemon zest.

For buttered oranges, to accompany the ice, peel 6 satsumas and, leaving them whole, place on a foil square. Cut ¼ cup unsalted butter into 6 pieces and add a piece to each orange with 1 teaspoon light brown sugar and a pinch of ground cinnamon. Wrap the foil to enclose the ingredients, then put on a baking sheet and cook in a preheated oven, 350°F, for 10 minutes. Serve hot with scoops of ice.

coffee and hazelnut choc ices

Serves **6**

Preparation time **25 minutes**, plus freezing

Cooking time **5–10 minutes**

1 tablespoon **instant coffee**

2 tablespoons **boiling water**

4 **egg yolks**

¼ cup **superfine sugar**

3 tablespoons **liquid glucose**

1¼ cups **heavy cream**

4 oz **bittersweet chocolate**, broken into pieces

3 tablespoons **hazelnuts**, toasted and roughly chopped

4 tablespoons **Kahlua coffee liqueur** or **coffee cream liqueur**, to serve

Dissolve the coffee in the boiling water. Put the egg yolks, sugar, and liquid glucose in a large bowl set over a saucepan of simmering water and beat for 5–10 minutes until very thick and the mixture leaves a trail when the whisk is lifted. Take the bowl off the heat and stand in cold water, then beat until cool. Whip the cream in a second bowl until it forms soft swirls. Fold into the beaten yolks with the dissolved coffee.

Line an 8 inch shallow square cake pan with plastic wrap, covering the inside of the pan completely. Pour in the coffee mixture and freeze for 3 hours until firm.

Melt the chocolate (see page 11) over a pan of gently simmering water. Spoon onto a baking sheet lined with nonstick parchment paper and spread into a thin even layer. Sprinkle with hazelnuts and chill until firm.

Lift out the coffee ice using the plastic wrap. Cut the ice into 3 even-size strips, then cut each strip into 4 rectangles. Cut the chocolate into slightly larger pieces, then lift off the paper with a spatula.

Layer 3 chocolate rectangles with 2 rectangles of coffee ice in between to make 6 stacks. Put one stack on each serving plate, then drizzle the liqueur around the plate. Serve at once.

For double chocolate ices, follow the recipe above but replace the coffee with 4 oz melted bittersweet chocolate. Spoon into ramekin dishes lined with plastic wrap and freeze until firm. Serve on plates drizzled with chocolate sauce (see page 172), topped with a few chocolate curls (see page 11).

iced chocolate mousses

Serves **6**

Preparation time **30 minutes**, plus cooling and freezing

Cooking time **10 minutes**

8 oz **bittersweet chocolate**

1 tablespoon **unsalted butter**

2 tablespoons **liquid glucose**

3 tablespoons **fresh orange juice**

3 **eggs**, separated

¾ cup **heavy cream**

Make chocolate curls by paring the underside of the block of chocolate with a swivel-bladed vegetable peeler. If the curls are very small, microwave the chocolate in 10-second bursts on full power (or place in a warm oven) until the chocolate is soft enough to shape. When you have enough curls to decorate 6 mousses, break the remainder into pieces—you should have about 7 oz—and melt (see page 11).

Stir the butter and glucose into the chocolate, then mix in the orange juice. Stir the yolks one by one into the mix until smooth. Take off the heat and let cool.

Beat the egg whites until softly peaking. Whip the cream until it forms soft swirls. Fold the cream, then the egg whites, into the chocolate mix. Pour the mixture into 6 coffee cups or ramekin dishes.

Freeze for 4 hours or overnight until firm. Decorate the tops with chocolate curls.

For chilled chocolate & coffee mousses, omit the chocolate curls and liquid glucose. Melt 7 oz bittersweet chocolate, then add 1 tablespoon butter, 3 tablespoons strong black coffee, and 3 egg yolks. Fold in 3 beaten egg whites, then pour into 4 small dishes or glasses and chill in the refrigerator for 4 hours until set. Whip ½ cup heavy cream until it forms soft swirls, then fold in 2 tablespoons coffee cream liqueur, if desired. Spoon on top of the mousses and decorate with a little sifted cocoa powder.

honeyed banana ice cream

Serves **4–6**
Preparation time **15 minutes**,
  plus freezing and setting

1 lb **bananas**
2 tablespoons **lemon juice**
3 tablespoons **honey**
⅔ cup **plain yogurt**
⅔ cup **chopped nuts**
⅔ cup **heavy cream**
2 **egg whites**

Praline
3 tablespoons **water**
¾ cup **superfine sugar**
2 tablespoons **corn syrup**
1¼ cups **toasted almonds**

Put the bananas in a bowl with the lemon juice and mash until smooth. Stir in the honey, followed by the yogurt and nuts, and beat well. Place the banana mix and the cream in an ice-cream machine. Churn and freeze following the manufacturer's instructions until half frozen. Alternatively, whip the cream until it forms soft swirls, then fold into the banana mix and freeze in a plastic container for 3–4 hours until partially frozen.

Beat the egg whites lightly until they form soft peaks. Add to the ice-cream machine and continue to churn and freeze until completely frozen. Alternatively, break up the ice cream in the plastic container with a fork, then fold in the beaten egg white and freeze until firm.

Make the praline. Pour the measured water into a heavy saucepan and add the sugar and corn syrup. Simmer gently until the sugar has dissolved, then cook to a caramel-colored syrup. Place the toasted almonds on a lightly greased piece of foil and pour the syrup over. Allow to set for 1 hour. Once set, break up into irregular pieces and serve with the ice cream.

For honeyed banana ice cream with sticky glazed bananas, make the ice cream as above. When ready to serve, heat 2 tablespoons unsalted butter in a skillet, add 3 thickly sliced bananas, and fry until just beginning to soften. Sprinkle with 3 tablespoons light brown sugar and cook until dissolved and the bananas are browning around the edges. Add the grated zest and juice of 1 lime, cook for 1 minute, then serve with the ice cream.

white choc & raspberry castles

Serves **6**

Preparation time **30 minutes**,
  plus freezing

3 cups **strawberry ice cream**
8 oz **white chocolate**, broken
  into pieces
3 cups **raspberries**

Line 6 small straight-sided individual china dishes or metal pudding molds with plastic wrap, then press a thick layer of ice cream into the base of each, then top with two small scoops. Freeze for 2–3 hours until firm.

Melt the chocolate (see page 11). Cut 6 strips of paper the circumference of the dish or mold and 1 inch higher than the top of the dish or mold. Spread the chocolate over the paper strips so that it covers the base and two short ends with a wavy, jagged edge to the second long side, just in from the paper edge.

Lift the ice cream quickly out of the molds using the plastic wrap, then peel off the plastic wrap. Wrap one of the chocolate-covered strips around the side of the refrozen ice cream so that the chocolate touches the ice cream and the paper is on the outside. Repeat with the other molded ice creams. Return to the freezer for 2 hours.

Reserve a few raspberries to decorate each castle. Puree the remainder of the raspberries and sieve, if desired. Drizzle the puree over 6 serving plates. Remove the ice creams from the freezer and peel away the paper. Transfer a castle to the center of each serving plate and decorate with a few raspberries.

For brandy snap baskets with summer berries, use 3 cups frozen mixed summer berry fruits instead of the raspberries. Reserve half the fruit and puree the rest, drizzling over 6 serving plates. Instead of making the castles, put the remaining fruit in 6 bought brandy-snap baskets and arrange on the plates with a scoop each of vanilla ice cream. Decorate with mint leaves.

key lime pie

Serves **8**

Preparation time **30 minutes**, plus chilling

Cooking time **15–20 minutes**

2½ cups crushed **graham crackers**

4 tablespoons **superfine sugar**

6 tablespoons **unsalted butter**, melted

3 **eggs**, separated

1⅓ cups **full-fat condensed milk**

½ cup freshly squeezed **lime juice**

1 tablespoon **lemon juice**

2 teaspoons grated **lime zest**

Topping

1 cup **heavy cream**

1 tablespoon **confectioners' sugar**

vanilla extract

lime slices, to decorate (optional)

Combine the cracker crumbs, half the sugar, and the melted butter and press over the bottom and up the sides of a greased 9 inch springform pan. Refrigerate while making the filling.

Beat the egg yolks lightly together until creamy. Add the condensed milk, lime and lemon juice, and lime zest and beat until well mixed and slightly thickened. In another bowl, beat the egg whites until stiff. Add the remainder of the sugar and continue beating until the meringue holds soft peaks (see page 10). Use a large metal spoon to fold the meringue mixture gently but thoroughly into the lime mixture.

Spoon the filling into the crumb crust and smooth the top. Bake the pie in a preheated oven, 325°F, for 15–20 minutes or until the filling is just firm and lightly browned on top. When cool, refrigerate the pie for at least 3 hours, until it is well chilled.

Whip the cream until it begins to thicken. Add the confectioners' sugar and vanilla extract and continue whipping until it forms thick swirls. Spread the cream over the top of the chilled pie. Decorate with twisted lime slices, if desired. Remove the side of the pan just before serving and serve well chilled.

For no-bake key lime pie, make the crumb crust as above. Whip 1¼ cups heavy cream until it forms soft swirls. Fold in 1⅓ cups condensed milk, then beat in the grated zest and juice of 3 limes until thick. Pour into the crumb shell, spread into an even layer, then chill for at least 4 hours. Serve sliced, sprinkled with lime zest curls.

last-minute quickies

chocolate apple crêpes

Serves **4**
Preparation time **10 minutes**
Cooking time **7–8 minutes**

3 tablespoons **unsalted
butter**
3 **dessert apples**, cored and
thickly sliced
2 large pinches **ground
cinnamon**
4 **ready-made crêpes**, about
8 inches in diameter
4 tablespoons **chocolate and
hazelnut spread**
confectioners' sugar, for
dusting

Melt half the butter in a large skillet, then add the
apples and fry for 3–4 minutes, stirring and turning
until hot and lightly browned. Sprinkle with cinnamon.

Separate the crêpes, then spread with chocolate
spread. Divide the apples among the crêpes, spooning
them on to cover half of each crêpe. Fold the uncovered
sides over the apples.

Heat the remaining butter in the skillet, add the crêpes,
and fry for a couple of minutes on each side to warm
the crêpes through. Transfer to shallow plates and dust
with sifted confectioners' sugar.

For peach melba crêpes, fry 2 large, thickly sliced
peaches in the butter instead of the apples, omitting
the cinnamon. Spread the crêpes with 4 tablespoons
raspberry jelly, then add the peaches and fold. Warm
through as above, then serve sprinkled with fresh
raspberries, a dusting of confectioners' sugar, and a
scoop of ice cream.

poached peaches & raspberries

Serves **6**
Preparation time **15 minutes**
Cooking time **25 minutes**

1 cup **water**
⅔ cup **marsala** or **sweet sherry**
⅓ cup **superfine sugar**
1 **vanilla bean**
6 **peaches**, halved and pitted
1¼ cups **fresh raspberries**

Pour the measured water and marsala or sherry into a saucepan, then add the sugar. Slit the vanilla bean lengthwise and scrape out the black seeds from inside the pod. Add these to the water with the pod, then gently heat the mixture until the sugar has dissolved.

Place the peach halves in an overproof dish so that they sit together snugly. Pour over the hot syrup, then cover and cook in a preheated oven, 350°F, for 20 minutes.

Scatter over the raspberries. Serve the fruit either warm or cold. Spoon into serving bowls and decorate with the vanilla bean cut into thin strips.

For poached prunes with vanilla, make the sugar syrup as above, then add 1½ cups dried pitted prunes instead of the peaches. Cover and simmer as above, then serve warm with spoonfuls of sour cream and 4 crumbled amaretti cookies.

tamarind & mango sundae

Serves **4**

Preparation time **10 minutes**,
  plus cooling

Cooking time **8 minutes**

1 tablespoon **tamarind paste**
⅛ cup **light brown sugar**
2 tablespoons **corn syrup**
grated zest and juice of **1 lime**,
  plus extra pared **lime zest**,
  to decorate (optional)
⅔ cup **water**
2 teaspoons **cornstarch**
1 tablespoon **unsalted butter**
1 large **mango**, pitted, peeled,
  and cut into strips
12 scoops **vanilla ice cream**

Put the tamarind paste, sugar, and corn syrup in a small saucepan. Add the lime zest and juice and the measured water and bring to a boil, stirring until the sugar has dissolved. Simmer for 5 minutes.

Mix the cornstarch with a little extra water in a cup, then add to the sauce with the butter, bring back to a boil and heat, stirring until thickened. Set aside to cool for 10 minutes.

Divide the mango and ice cream between 4 glass dishes, then drizzle a little of the sauce over the top and decorate with extra lime zest curls, if desired. Serve the remaining sauce in a small pitcher.

For tamarind & banana yogurts, make the tamarind sauce as above and leave until completely cold. Roughly chop 3 bananas and mix with 1¾ cups Greek or whole milk yogurt. Add the cooled tamarind sauce and mix briefly for a marbled effect. Spoon into glass dishes and serve.

pain perdu with mixed berries

Serves **4**
Preparation time **10 minutes**
Cooking time **10 minutes**

4 thick slices **brioche**
2 **eggs**
6 tablespoons **milk**
¼ cup **unsalted butter**
⅔ cup **Greek** or **whole milk yogurt**
2 cups **raspberries**
1 cup **blueberries**
confectioners' sugar, for dusting, or **maple syrup**

Cut each slice of brioche into two triangles. Beat the eggs and milk in a shallow bowl with a fork.

Heat half the butter in a skillet. Quickly dip the bread, a triangle at a time, into the egg mixture, then put as many as you can get into the skillet. Cook over a moderate heat until the underside is golden. Turn over and cook the second side, then lift out of the pan and keep hot.

Heat the remaining butter in the pan and dip and cook the remaining brioche triangles.

Arrange 2 triangles per serving on plates, top with spoonfuls of yogurt, a sprinkling of berries, and a light dusting of sifted confectioners' sugar or a drizzle of maple syrup. Serve immediately.

For spiced pain perdu with apricots, simmer 1 cup ready-to-eat dried apricots with the juice of 1 orange and ½ cup water for 10 minutes until tender. Cut 4 slices of fruit bread in half. Mix the egg and milk as above with ¼ teaspoon ground cinnamon, then dip and fry the fruit bread as above. Arrange on plates with ⅔ cup yogurt and warm apricot compote.

green fruit salad

Serves **6**

Preparation time **15 minutes**

1½ cups **seedless green grapes**, halved

4 **kiwifruits**, peeled, quartered, and sliced

2 ripe **pears,** peeled, cored, and sliced

4 **passion fruits**, halved

4 tablespoons **concentrated elderflower cordial**

4 tablespoons **water**

1¼ cups **Greek** or **whole milk yogurt**

2 tablespoons **honey**

Put the grapes, kiwifruits, and pears in a bowl. Using a teaspoon, scoop the seeds from 3 of the passion fruits into the bowl. Mix 2 tablespoons of the cordial with the measured water and drizzle over the salad. Gently toss together and spoon into 6 glass tumblers.

Stir the remaining undiluted cordial into the yogurt, then mix in the honey. Spoon into the glasses. Decorate with the remaining passion fruit seeds and serve.

For ruby fruit salad, mix 1½ cups halved seedless red grapes with 1¼ cups fresh raspberries and 1 cup sliced strawberries. Sprinkle with the seeds from ½ pomegranate, then drizzle with 6 tablespoons red grape juice. Mix the yogurt with honey only, then spoon over the fruit salad. Decorate with a few extra pomegranate seeds.

sweet soufflé omelet

Serves **4**
Preparation time **15 minutes**
Cooking time **10 minutes**

2¼ cups **strawberries**, hulled
and thickly sliced, plus extra
to decorate
2 tablespoons **red currant
jelly**
2 teaspoons **balsamic
vinegar**
5 **eggs**, separated
4 tablespoons **confectioners'
sugar**, sifted
2 tablespoons **unsalted
butter**

Warm the strawberries, red currant jelly, and vinegar together in a saucepan until the jelly has just melted.

Meanwhile, beat the egg whites into stiff, moist-looking peaks. Mix the egg yolks with 1 tablespoon of the sugar, then fold into the egg whites.

Heat the butter in a large skillet, add the egg mixture, and cook over a medium heat for 3–4 minutes until the underside is golden. Quickly transfer the pan to a hot broiler and cook for 2–3 minutes until the top is browned and the center still slightly soft, making sure that the pan handle is away from the heat.

Spoon the warm strawberry mixture over the omelet, fold in half, and dust with the remaining sugar. Cut into 4 and serve immediately with extra strawberries.

For sweet soufflé omelet with peaches & blueberries, put 2 ripe peaches, sliced, into a saucepan together with 1 cup blueberries, 2 tablespoons red currant jelly, and 2 tablespoons lemon juice. Warm together, then make the sweet soufflé omelet as above, spoon over the warm fruit, and serve immediately.

white choc & raspberry tiramisu

Serves **6**
Preparation time **20 minutes**

3 level teaspoons **instant coffee**
7 tablespoons **confectioners' sugar**
1 cup **boiling water**
12 **ladyfingers**, about 4 oz
1 cup **mascarpone cheese**
⅔ cup **heavy cream**
3 tablespoons **kirsch** (optional)
2 cups **fresh raspberries**
3 oz **white chocolate**, diced

Put the coffee and 4 tablespoons of the confectioners' sugar into a shallow dish, then pour on the measured boiling water and mix until dissolved. Dip 6 ladyfingers, one at a time, into the coffee mixture, then crumble into the bases of 6 glass tumblers.

Put the mascarpone into a bowl with the remaining confectioners' sugar, then gradually beat in the cream until smooth. Stir in the kirsch, if using, then divide half the mixture between the glasses.

Crumble half the raspberries over the top of the mascarpone in the glasses, then sprinkle with half the chocolate. Dip the remaining ladyfingers in the coffee mix, crumble, and add to the glasses. Then add the rest of the mascarpone and the remaining raspberries, this time left whole, finishing with a sprinkling of the chocolate. Serve immediately or chill until required.

For classic tiramisu, omit the raspberries and white chocolate from the layers. Mix the mascarpone with the cream and 3 tablespoons Kahlua coffee liqueur or brandy, then layer the mixture in one large glass dish with the coffee-dipped ladyfingers and 3 oz diced bittersweet chocolate.

banana ripples

Serves **4**
Preparation time **5 minutes**,
  plus standing

2 ripe **bananas**
juice of ½ **lemon**
1½ tablespoons finely chopped
  candied ginger, plus extra to
  decorate
⅔ cup **low-fat plain yogurt**
8 teaspoons **dark brown**
  sugar

Toss the bananas in a little lemon juice and mash on a plate with a fork. Add the ginger and yogurt and mix together. Spoon one-third of the mixture into the bases of 4 small dessert glasses.

Sprinkle 1 teaspoon of the sugar over each dessert. Spoon half of the remaining banana mixture on top, then repeat with a second layer of sugar. Complete the layers with the remaining banana mixture and decorate with a little extra ginger, cut into slightly larger pieces.

Allow the desserts to stand for 10–15 minutes for the sugar to dissolve and form a syrupy layer between the layers of banana yogurt. Serve with dainty cookies, if desired.

For banana, apricot, & cardamom ripples, cook ½ cup ready-to-eat dried apricots with ⅔ cup water and 2 roughly crushed cardamom pods, adding the pods and their black seeds, in a covered saucepan for 10 minutes until tender. Remove and discard the cardamom pods, then puree the mixture with 3 tablespoons fresh orange juice. Cool, then layer with banana and the yogurt mix as above. This can be served immediately.

summer fruit gratin

Serves **4**
Preparation time **10 minutes**
Cooking time **20 minutes**

2 ripe **peaches**, pitted
   and sliced
4 ripe **red plums**, pitted
   and sliced
1¼ cups mixed **raspberries**
   and **blackberries** (or all
   raspberries)
¾ cup **mascarpone cheese**
4 tablespoons **superfine
   sugar**
2 tablespoons **heavy cream**
grated zest of 1 **lime**

Arrange all the fruit in a shallow ovenproof dish. Mix the mascarpone with 2 tablespoons of the sugar, the cream, and the lime zest, then spoon over the fruit and spread into an even layer.

Sprinkle the top with the remaining sugar, then put on a baking sheet and cook in a preheated oven, 375°F, for 15 minutes until the cheese has softened and the sugar topping has caramelized. Serve immediately.

For tropical fruit gratin, replace the peaches, plums and berries with 1 large mango and 1 papaya, both sliced, and 1½ cups blueberries. Top with the mascarpone mix and bake as above.

baked apple & oat crumble

Serves **4**
Preparation time **15 minutes**
Cooking time **20–25 minutes**

4 **dessert apples**, halved and
  cored
½ cup **raisins**
4 tablespoons **corn syrup**
6 tablespoons **apple juice**
  or **water**
½ cup **all-purpose flour**
½ cup **rolled oats**
¼ cup **light brown sugar**
¼ cup **unsalted butter**, at
  room temperature, diced
2 tablespoons **sunflower
  seeds**
2 tablespoons **sesame seeds**

Arrange the apples, cut side up, in a shallow ovenproof
dish. Divide the raisins among the apples, pressing
them into the core cavity. Drizzle with 2 tablespoons
of the corn syrup and add the apple juice or water
to the base of the dish.

Put the flour, oats, sugar, and butter into a small bowl
and blend in the butter with fingertips until the mixture
resembles fine bread crumbs. Stir in the seeds. Spoon
the crumble over the top of the apples and mound up.
Drizzle with the remaining syrup.

Cook in a preheated oven, 350°F, for 20–25 minutes
until the crumble is golden and the apples are soft.
Serve the crumble warm with scoops of vanilla ice
cream or crème fraîche.

For plum & granola crumble, halve 10 plums and
place them, cut side up, in an ovenproof dish. Drizzle
with 2 tablespoons honey and add 6 tablespoons red
grape juice or water to the base of the dish. Make the
crumble, using 1 cup of granola instead of the oats
and seeds. Bake and serve as above.

hot caribbean fruit salad

Serves **4**
Preparation time **15 minutes**
Cooking time **6–7 minutes**

¼ cup **unsalted butter**
¼ cup **light brown sugar**
1 large **papaya**, halved,
  seeded, peeled, and sliced
1 large **mango**, pitted, peeled,
  and sliced
½ **pineapple**, cored, peeled,
  and cut into chunks
1¾ cups **full-fat coconut milk**
grated zest and juice of **1 lime**

Heat the butter in a large skillet, add the sugar, and heat gently until just dissolved. Add all the fruit and cook for 2 minutes, then pour in the coconut milk, half the lime zest, and all the juice.

Heat gently for 4–5 minutes, then serve warm in shallow bowls, sprinkled with the remaining lime zest.

For flamed Caribbean fruit salad, omit the coconut milk and add 3 tablespoons dark or white rum. When the rum is bubbling, flame with a long match and stand well back. When the flames have subsided, add the lime zest and juice and serve with scoops of vanilla ice cream.

mini baked alaskas

Serves **4**

Preparation time **15 minutes**,
  plus freezing time

Cooking time **5 minutes**

4 slices **jelly roll** or
  4 slices **pound cake**, with
  the corners trimmed off

4 scoops **strawberry and
  vanilla ice cream** or **vanilla
  ice cream**

2 **egg whites**

¼ cup **superfine sugar**

1 cup **frozen summer fruits**,
  just defrosted or warmed in
  a small saucepan

Arrange the slices of jelly roll or pound cake, well spaced apart, on a baking sheet, then top each with a scoop of ice cream. Put into the freezer for 10 minutes (or longer if you have time).

Beat the egg whites in a large bowl until stiff, moist-looking peaks form. Gradually beat in the sugar, a teaspoon at a time, and continue beating for a few minutes until thick and glossy (see page 10).

Take the cake and ice cream from the freezer and quickly swirl the meringue over the top and sides to cover completely. Cook in a preheated oven, 400°F, for 5 minutes until the peaks are golden brown, the meringue is cooked through, and the ice cream only just beginning to soften.

Transfer the baked Alaskas to shallow serving bowls and spoon the summer fruit around the base of the desserts. Serve immediately.

For cappuccino Alaskas, use chocolate roll (choose one without a chocolate outside coating) instead of the jelly roll or pound cake. Top each slice with a scoop of coffee ice cream, then the meringue as above. When baked, dust lightly with sifted instant cocoa powder, and serve immediately.

caramelized clementines with bay

Serves **4**
Preparation time **10 minutes**
Cooking time **12 minutes**

1 cup **granulated sugar**
1 cup **cold water**
8 **clementines**
4 small **fresh bay leaves**
6 tablespoons **boiling water**

Put the sugar and measured cold water in a saucepan and heat gently, stirring very occasionally until the sugar has completely dissolved.

Meanwhile, peel the clementines and, leaving them whole, place in a heavy glass serving bowl or mixing bowl with the bay leaves.

Increase the heat once the sugar has dissolved and boil the syrup for 8–10 minutes, without stirring and keeping a close watch on it until it begins to change color, first becoming pale golden around the edges, then a rich golden color all over.

Take the pan off the heat, then add the measured boiling water, a tablespoon at a time, standing well back in case the syrup spits. Tilt the pan to mix but don't stir. Once the bubbles have subsided, pour the hot syrup over the clementines and bay leaves. Allow to cool, then serve the dessert with scoops of crème fraîche or cream.

For caramelized clementines with whole spices, omit the bay leaves and add 2 whole star anise or the equivalent in pieces, 1 cinnamon stick, halved, and 3 cloves to the clementines. Make the syrup as above, then pour it over the spices and fruit.

mulled wine pears

Serves **6**
Preparation time **10 minutes**
Cooking time **12 minutes**

1¼ cups cheap **red wine**
¾ cup **water**
rind and juice of **1 orange**
1 cinnamon stick, broken into
   large pieces
6 cloves
2 small **fresh bay leaves**
⅓ cup **superfine sugar**
6 pears
3 teaspoons **cornstarch**

Pour the wine and measured water into a saucepan that will hold the pears snugly. Cut the orange zest into thin strips, then add to the pan with the orange juice, spices, bay leaves, and sugar. Heat gently until the sugar has dissolved.

Peel the pears, leaving the stalks on, then add them to the red wine syrup. Simmer gently for 10 minutes, turning the pears several times so that they cook and color evenly.

Lift the pears out of the pan and put on a plate. Mix the cornstarch with a little water in a cup, then stir into the wine syrup and bring to a boil, stirring until thickened and smooth. Add the pears and allow to cool.

Transfer to shallow dishes with a rim and serve with spoonfuls of crème fraîche or cream.

For apples with cider punch, use hard cider in place of the red wine, then add the orange zest and juice, spices, and sugar as above, omitting the bay leaves. Dissolve the sugar, then add 6 dessert apples, peeled, cored, and quartered. Simmer for 5 minutes until just tender, then thicken the syrup with cornstarch as described above.

moroccan baked figs with yogurt

Serves **4**
Preparation time **10 minutes**
Cooking time **10 minutes**

8 **fresh figs**, rinsed in cold
 water
about 3 teaspoons **rose water**
4 tablespoons **honey**
¼ cup **unsalted butter**
1 cup **Greek** or **whole milk**
 yogurt
a little **Turkish delight**, roughly
 chopped

Cut a cross in the top of each fig and open out the cut
to halfway through the fruit. Arrange the figs in a small
roasting pan or shallow ovenproof dish. Add a few
drops of rose water to each fig, then drizzle with
3 tablespoons of the honey and dot with the butter.

Bake in a preheated oven, 375°F, for 8–10 minutes
until the figs are hot but still firm. Meanwhile, mix the
yogurt with the remaining honey and gradually mix in a
little of the remaining rose water to taste.

Transfer the figs to shallow serving dishes and serve
with spoonfuls of yogurt sprinkled with Turkish delight.

For orange & pistachio baked apricots, arrange
12 fresh apricots, halved, in a roasting pan. Add a few
drops of orange flower water to each apricot half, then
drizzle with 3 tablespoons honey and sprinkle with
⅓ cup halved pistachio nuts. Dot with ¼ cup butter
and bake as above. Serve with 1 cup Greek or whole
milk yogurt flavored with 1 tablespoon honey and
orange flower water to taste.

white chocolate fondue with fruit

Serves **4**
Preparation time **10 minutes**
Cooking time **5 minutes**

7 oz good-quality **white chocolate**, broken into pieces
1¼ cups **heavy cream**
2 tablespoons **kirsch**
2 **peaches**, cut into chunks
2 cups large **raspberries**
2 cups **strawberries**, halved
small bunch of **seedless red grapes**

Melt the chocolate together with the cream in a bowl set over a pan of gently simmering water (see page 11). Stir in the kirsch.

Arrange all the fruit on individual serving plates with forks or skewers for spearing the pieces.

Keep the fondue warm over a fondue burner while you dip and eat, or spoon the fondue into individual bowls, if preferred.

For dark chocolate & vanilla fondue, heat 7 oz bittersweet chocolate, 1¼ cups heavy cream, 4 tablespoons light brown sugar, and 1 teaspoon vanilla extract together, stirring until smooth. Serve with 2 peaches, cut into chunks, 2 red-skinned dessert apples, cut into chunks, and about 16 marshmallows.

broiled strawberry zabaglione

Serves **4**
Preparation time **10 minutes**
Cooking time **10 minutes**

3 cups **strawberries**, halved
   or quartered, depending on
   size
3 **egg yolks**
¼ cup **superfine sugar**
6 tablespoons **dry** or **sweet**
   sherry
4 teaspoons **confectioners'**
   sugar

Divide the strawberries among 4 shallow 1¼ cup ovenproof dishes, or use a large 5 cup dish if preferred.

Put the egg yolks, sugar, and 4 tablespoons of the sherry in a large bowl and set over a pan of simmering water. Cook the mixture, beating continuously using a hand-held electric mixer (or rotary hand or balloon whisk), for 5 minutes until the mixture is very thick and frothy and almost half-fills the bowl.

Add the remaining sherry and cook for a few more minutes until thick once more. Pour the mixture over the strawberries and sift the confectioners' sugar over the top.

Cook under a preheated hot broiler for 3–4 minutes until golden or caramelize the sugar with a kitchen torch. Serve immediately.

For fruit salad zabaglione, divide 1 cup fresh raspberries, ½ cup halved seedless red or green grapes, and 2 peeled and diced kiwifruits among 4 glass tumblers. Make the zabaglione with 6 tablespoons dry white wine instead of sherry, and when just cooked pour over the fruit but don't broil.

caramelized blueberries & custard

Serves **6**
Preparation time **10 minutes**
Cooking time **5 minutes**

⅔ cup **granulated sugar**
3 tablespoons **cold water**
2 tablespoons **boiling water**
1½ cups **fresh** (not frozen)
   blueberries
1¾ cups **fromage frais** or
   plain yogurt
14 oz can or carton **custard**

Put the sugar and measured cold water into a skillet and heat gently, stirring very occasionally until the sugar has completely dissolved. Bring to a boil and cook for 3–4 minutes, without stirring, until the syrup is just changing color and is golden around the edges.

Add the measured boiling water, standing well back as the syrup will spit, then tilt the pan to mix. Add the blueberries and cook for 1 minute. Take the pan off the heat and set aside to cool slightly (maybe while you eat your main course).

Mix the fromage frais or yogurt and custard together, spoon into small dishes, then spoon the blueberry mixture over the top. Serve immediately, with baby meringues if desired.

For banana custards, make the caramel as above, then add 2 sliced bananas instead of the blueberries. Cool slightly, then spoon over the custard and fromage frais or yogurt mixture. Decorate with a little grated bittersweet chocolate.

citrus refresher

Serves **4**
Preparation time **10 minutes**
Cooking time **6–7 minutes**

⅔ cup chilled **orange juice**
  from a carton
⅔ cup **water**
½ cup **superfine sugar**
juice of ½ **lemon**
2 **ruby grapefruit**
4 **oranges** (a mix of **ordinary**
  and **blood oranges**, if
  available)
1 **orange-fleshed melon**
½ **pomegranate**

Pour the orange juice and measured water into a saucepan, add the sugar, and heat gently until the sugar has dissolved, then simmer for 5 minutes until syrupy. Take off the heat and mix in the lemon juice.

Cut a slice off the top and bottom of each grapefruit, then cut away the rest of the peel in downward slices using a small serrated knife. Holding the fruit over a bowl, cut between the membranes to release the segments. Cut a slice off the top and bottom of the oranges, then cut away the rest of the peel. Cut into segments and add to the bowl.

Cut the melon in half, scoop out the seeds, then cut away the peel and dice the flesh. Add to the citrus fruit, then pour over the syrup. Flex the pomegranate to release the seeds, sprinkle over the salad, then chill until ready to serve.

For orange & fig refresher, make the syrup as above. Omit the grapefruit and increase the number of oranges to 6. Cut 4 fresh figs into wedges, peel, and add to the oranges. Add the sugar syrup and sprinkle with some fresh mint leaves. Serve chilled.

barbecued bananas

Serves **4**
Preparation time **5 minutes**
Cooking time **10 minutes**

4 **bananas**
4 tablespoons **rum** (or
　Amaretto liqueur, **brandy**,
　or **sherry**)
grated zest of 1 **lime**

To serve
4 scoops **vanilla ice cream**
·8 **ratafia cookies**, crumbled

Cook the bananas still in their skins on the barbecue for 8–10 minutes as the heat from the embers begins to lose its fierceness, until the skins have blackened and the flesh is softened. Alternatively, bake for the same period in a preheated oven, 400°F.

Split the skins lengthwise and place a banana in its skin on each of 4 serving plates. Drizzle the rum inside the baked banana and sprinkle with the lime zest. Serve at once, with scoops of ice cream and the crumbled ratafia cookies.

For Jamaican banana parcels, peel 4 bananas, halve lengthwise, and divide between 4 pieces of foil. Dot with 3 tablespoons unsalted butter, 2 tablespoons light brown sugar, the juice of 1 lime, and 2 tablespoons rum. Seal the foil well so that none of the ingredients can escape, then add to the barbecue and cook for 5–8 minutes until the bananas are softened. Serve warm with ice cream.

index

acknowledgments

Executive Editor: Nicola Hill
Senior Editor: Fiona Robertson
Executive Art Editor: Leigh Jones
Designer: Jo Tapper
Photographer: Will Heap
Home Economist: Sara Lewis
Props Stylist: Liz Hippisley
Production Controller: Carolin Stransky

Special Photography: © Octopus Publishing Group Limited/Will Heap
Other Photography: © Octopus Publishing Group Limited/Gareth Sambridge 20, 22, 29, 35, 49, 73, 125, 151, 179; /Ian Wallace 81, 85, 89, 93, 97, 101, 107, 121, 126, 127, 131, 183, 193; /Jeremy Hopley 143, 147; /Lis Parsons 77, 135, 139, 154, 208; /Stephen Conroy 111, 169, 173, 177, 188; /William Lingwood 105.